THE WAY BACK HOME

THE ABE CONVERSATIONS

Volume 1

THE WAY BACK HOME

THE ABE CONVERSATIONS

TWBH

TheWayBackHome Publishing

Published by TheWayBackHome Publishing –

https://www.thewaybackhome.one/

ISBN-13: 978-1-9993440-8-5 (paperback)

First published: October 2019

Book Design & Formatting – S.J. & B.S.

WHO WE ARE

NM allows the ABE communications to flow and has been writing them down for a number of years. KD has the great pleasure of formulating the questions (mostly!) and of formatting the answers into punctuated sentences. ABE-NM-KD are a triad that flow together.

NM

NM first started receiving the ABE communications back in 2007. They came as 'nudges' in the beginning, but over time developed into the written communications like we have today. With the help of KD the connection to ABE has strengthened and developed. NM is a mother of four and a small business owner, living on the coast of Wales. She hopes to continue to grow within herself, and also strengthen this connection to ABE within this triad of being.

KD

KD worked for many years in the educational sector, teaching at various schools and universities in England and overseas. He left academia in late 2008 to continue as an independent freelance researcher and writer. He has published over a dozen books, including non-fiction, adult and children's fiction, poetry, essays, and plays. He lives in the countryside and likes to grow his own food where possible.

Introduction – from NM

ABE was not something out of the blue that suddenly happened, that connected from out of nowhere. It had been knocking at the perceptual door for some time, but many a time I chose to ignore it. Why I don't know - I felt it was weird, that maybe I didn't understand it, and also quite fearful of it too. I think we all fear that in which we don't know. At some point though we have to open up that perceptual door and allow the unknown, allow ourselves, allow life.

I felt from a small child that I had a different sense. That I could pick up on things that others couldn't or would seemingly ignore. Looking back, I feel I have had continuous nudges, but I chose to either ignore it or push it aside, not knowing what it was I was getting. The first time I had a so-called 'nudge' was when I moved in 2007. I felt things change for me in the sense of my perceptions. Now a nudge is something I get when I feel compelled to write something (as I do now) or something that I feel needs to be spoken; you would perhaps call it an intuitive nudge.

However, for me, it feels different (or maybe it doesn't, perhaps it's the same for everyone?) I feel that this is not my thinking but something apart from my own perceptions, but also at the same time not separate - confusing? That's exactly how I felt. As time went on, I started to get more of these nudges, so I decided to give it more of my attention. I went to psychics to try and get answers as to why I was getting this. They mostly said that I too was psychic, that I should nurture this connection, saying it was a spirit or my guides. However, something about all that didn't seem to fit for me. At this point I didn't know what to believe, I just knew that that wasn't right in some way. I became close to a lady who happened to be psychic, and she offered to help me develop, but it never seemed to fit correctly. I was either scared, or I just felt foolish doing it. I guess in my mind I didn't want to give people false hope or information if I didn't quite believe it myself. There was something that I got from it all though, and it was from my friend - she said to write what comes. I did, I had a go, albeit very briefly, then closed it down again and shut it out mainly through fear - fear of what others would think and also fear of not knowing, of not being confident enough in myself to proceed with it.

In 2011 I decided to connect again, this is the time that I got the name ABE and that it was a collective and it spoke for many. This scared me a little if I'm honest. I didn't know how to deal with it. What I was taping into, and how I should handle it - part of me just wanted to flow with it, but again, fear got the better of me. I told my psychic friend, who scared me even more when she spoke of evil spirits and that I shouldn't mess around with it if I wasn't confident or knew enough. So once again, I closed it down. Time went on, and although there was a sense of this connection, I ignored it still. I had my youngest son and life went on normally or as normal as life could be. I still had nudges, but I chose to get on with it, and leave things alone that I didn't know enough about. But it was still there, lingering on my mind - questions of what this was and why me, etc.

I moved to Wales in 2013. Wales gave me such a new perspective, a new sense of being - but most of all, it gave me space. In this space I started writing bits. The first bits of ABE were, right from the beginning, questions mainly for myself and what I should be doing and what was I meant to do with this connection. They were exceptionally 'on and off' and were used more as a guidance. Yet even looking back at those first messages they had resonance with what is now: the answers were never personal as such - never of what I should do but whatever I was dealing with at the time it gave an overview, never really ever specific for me. From here on in I never shut it out again; well, not completely - like before. I never denied it again but toyed with it and continued to dabble.

In 2014 I met a lady, C, whom I shared the ABE stuff with. I rarely share it with anyone other than my husband, so it was good to share it and get another's take on it, finally. We didn't work with it straight away, as we had other projects going on together, so it was spoken of but not done anything with. As time went on, and other projects finished, we decided to look at the ABE material again. I made contact again, and this time it was said that there should be a question and answer book, and that the title should be THE WAY BACK HOME.

We made a virtual document and started gathering conversations, very similar to what we have now, but it was very sporadic, and the connection didn't feel deep. In the end, we did very little with it.

My first ever encounter of KD was, as I remember, reading an article in September 2018 that I came across on the Internet. I read the article and had such a strong sense to connect to the author. I found his email and wrote to him, in which he replied. We spoke for a while before I approached him with the ABE conversation writings that I had been having with C. I guess I was testing the waters with our connection, but something compelled me to send him some of the ABE material, despite me being extremely anxious about doing so. He was intrigued by it, which was a big relief as I had a deep draw to KD. I had a deep sense that I should be doing something with him, with the ABE material. What that was exactly was though was yet to be seen - but it felt like a good flow, a good sense to go with. I didn't want to let my friend C down, but I knew I had to trust what I was getting.

KD and I started the first set of conversations in October through an online virtual document that we had access to at the same time. I feel this connection with KD has deeply strengthened not only this connection to ABE but also to myself and back to that of KD - this 'Triad' of being. I am glad I decided to contact KD, and trust that what I was getting was correct and to follow it. There are not many things in life that I am sure of, but I am sure that this connection that we continue to strengthen, continue to grow, will be one thing that I can honestly look back on and say I'm glad I listened, I'm glad I finally acknowledged it. I feel incredibly blessed to be sharing this connection with others and also to being able to have this connection in the first place. I'm so glad it came together in the right way, with the right person.

How & What it feels like to connect

It's so hard to describe how I do it and what it feels like as it feels so natural; like I have allowed something to express finally - to flow. But I will do my best to say something. The way I write and connect with ABE is really just a dropping back, if you will - that is all I can describe it as, as if I put myself to the side. I feel like it is not me, it is a hearing but not of a hearing; then writing more so that they are coherent. They emerge mutually: something isn't spoken in my mind then written - it is jointly appearing, it's a flow. At the time of writing, I feel as if I fully understand that in which is being written, so it feels incredibly odd to read it back and not get it sometimes. I do not feel ABE as a being as such; there is no distinction of voice - it really does just feel like an allowance. Doing this connection now with KD, I realize there was never anything to be afraid of. I guess it all fell into place at the right time. I hope what we get can benefit others. I'm not sure as to where it will lead, or what is in store for this material; all we know is that it is something to continue to nurture - to continue to strengthen, and to continue to share with others that in which we get.

NM

Introduction – from KD

The ABE Material & Me

The Before

Okay, the best place to start is usually at the beginning. So that is where I shall begin – more or less. The first time I knew of NM was when I received an email out of the blue, sometime around early September 2018. She wrote to say that she had recently read an article of mine and something compelled her to get in touch. We corresponded on this topic and slowly, and courteously, began to discuss similar topics and articles. As I said to NM later, I always respond to such initial messages when people write to me – it's part of the grand network of unexpected contacts and occurrences. Who knows what will come of such encounters – who knows, indeed? (I did tell NM later on that there were no alarm bells ringing, so I was happy to continue our early messaging – to her amused relief!). We then moved onto messaging through social media and began corresponding in a more informal way - more like buddies. Anyway, at this time NM had enrolled at university to study philosophy, and her mind was naturally active on these topics. It didn't take us long to find out that not only had we been born in the same city in England, but that we had grown up just down the road from each other – literally, just a couple of miles between us. We had, it seemed, a common bond.

It was then that NM ventured a step further, and asked me, somewhat timidly, what I thought about life after death, and the idea that a part of us lives on, indefinitely. I say timidly, because NM wasn't sure how I would react to this. I reassured her that my mind was not only very open to such concepts, but that I had written a fair amount on issues such as collective and universal consciousness, the conscious universe, and multidimensional reality. This seemed to put her more at ease. And it was perhaps also the reason why NM ventured another step: 'You're going to think I'm weird or crazy, or something…but…' And here came the big but – there was something else NM wished to confide in me and to share. It was about a series of communications she said she had been receiving. Receiving? I asked. How do you mean by receiving? No, these were not communications by email but from a 'contact' or 'source' that NM could hear within herself. I was intrigued and asked her to tell me more. NM was very shy in this respect and was hesitant to say too much. I suspected she was wary that I might think her a weirdo. But far from it, NM seems to me to be one of the most down-to-Earth people I know. I encouraged her to send some of the material over to me, just to take a glance. I said I would look at them with an open mind.

In my research and reading I have come across several published communications that are known generically as 'channeling' or 'channeled material.' I even have several books on my bookshelf from various channeled contacts, whether they are from nearby star systems, or are classified as discarnate entities. I was open to delving into such material to see what 'words of wisdom' they may offer up. So, I made the bold step of agreeing to read some of these 'received communications.' And NM made the even bolder step of sending them across to me – the waters had broken.

I received an email containing the first of the received communications. It was at this point that I found out that NM had been calling the contact ABE. This was, she said, the name they had given her. NM didn't know herself why they chose this name; we only found out when we questioned them later on – as the book reveals. To begin, the first two things I realized when reading the initial ABE material was that firstly, it was all positive stuff – no fear mongering or messages of doom or end of the world type of stuff. On the contrary, all good positive-vibe material. And secondly, it was quite common sense and down-to-earth, as we say. That was a good start. Mm, I thought, NM might be on to something here. I immediately asked her to send me some more. NM was still hesitant and didn't seem entirely sure if I was being truthful at this stage or coaxing her on (it was, after all, in the early stages of our virtual friendship). NM sent me some material that were a series of questions and answers that she had done a few years previously with a female friend of hers. Then, it seems, NM had ceased with the contact. Why? I wondered. Why had NM not continued? I asked her – 'I dunno, really' came her non-committal response. She told me that things were going okay, yet perhaps there was a direction, an energy lacking. It seemed a shame to me that such an opportunity could not have been developed upon. After all, we never know where a path may lead a person, and what may open up from these pathways. After all, why had this unusual connection opened up between us now – strangers from the same neck-of-the-woods?

My response to NM from readings of the early ABE material was positive. ABE was speaking about maintaining our stability, our personal vibrations, and to steer towards unity. There was nothing I would consider strange, weird, or even cosmic about it. It was rather more about trying to be a stable human being! I think NM was relieved that I came back to her with an encouraging response, and that I didn't call her a wacky weirdo and immediately cease contact (now, that would have been a bit harsh). Anyway, that's not like me. Unusual things tend to happen for a reason – and it's all a matter of perspective. At this stage I was willing to keep my perspective open. Then NM ventured forth with another proposal, albeit in her timid way. Would I be interested in asking a few questions to ABE? Now, who could refuse such an offer? Not me.

And that's when it all began. And the rest is history, as they say. Well, not quite history yet – just the next step!

The During

Around late October NM and I agreed to meet online to do some questions for ABE. NM had a four-week semester break from her university studies and so it seemed a good time to put aside for focusing on the ABE contact. Since we were only in virtual contact, we thought it best to create an online document that could be shared by the both of us simultaneously. This would be a good way of being in touch with the answers as they came; and I could, if necessary, write any immediate follow-on questions (which often happened). We didn't really know where we might be heading, or what would materialize from the whole venture. Yet as they say — nothing ventured, nothing gained!

It was a Monday morning…that's all I remember. I couldn't say if it was sunny or rainy, or either what the exact date was — just late October 2018. And it began with my first question: **Hello Abe. Can you explain 'who' is Abe?**

Just who, or what, ABE is, is explained throughout these communications. I would also like to say that this is something which the reader shouldn't get too hung-up about. For me, the notion of communicating with the underlying collective consciousness — the zero-state — and the origin of everything before physical manifestation, is unique. It also fits well with the latest findings in our quantum sciences. Yet, at the end of the day, is this really the important point? Read the communications — and if they make sense and work for you, then trust in your own innate response to the communications. That, after all, is the important bit — not 'who' ABE is, but what 'they' have to communicate to you and me. Anyway, we had to begin with a first question — so we made it a 'who' one.

Then the rest of the questions followed in what I termed as 'Setting the Scene,' as you will see when you read this book. I didn't have any specific plan in mind. Most of the questions were planned out in advance. I would sit down and think them out, write them down, then transfer them to the online document for the next day's ABE meet-up. Yet there were also a good many questions that were asked directly as follow-up ones, once having read the answer to the previous question. These were then numbered in the order they were asked-answered, as presented in the book. There has been no shifting or changing of the order – all questions in the book appear in the chronological order in which they were asked.

In advance we decided upon certain themes we wished to address, once the 'setting the scene' was out of the way; such as consciousness, health, society, technology, the cosmos, the future, etc. In this, the questions were finally divided into sections so as to group themes together. Over three weeks and over two hundred questions later, we felt we had come to a natural end. We felt as if we had a wealth of material. What we needed to do now was read through it all – again – and to try to absorb what we had been offered.

I should say at this point that the way NM works is that she reads and 'mentalizes' a question, and then receives a response in her mind. How that works, and what that voice sounds like; well, only NM can explain that. What NM writes is in a continuous flow; that is, it has no punctuation – no full stops or apparent sentences. Why this is, I don't know. I wish it wasn't this way, as it would make my life easier. After each response I need to read through and format the words into grammatical sentences. This is not easy, as it is not always apparent where the break, or pause, should go. Is there a full-stop here? Are these two separate sentences? The combinations are various. I hope I have done a good job in piecing these communications into readable constructs. If not, then most of the blame lies with me (but not all – read section below on ABE style). When you are reading through this material, bear in mind that perhaps the sentences could have been formed in a different way. Maybe you wish to make your own grammatical combinations?

During these communications the connection between NM and myself developed as we had been quite literally strangers to one another - and with ABE too. Naturally, these communications created greater connection between us. ABE would say – and does say – we are all inherently connected in this way anyway; we've just forgotten this, and have de-synched away from this essential connection. So, if anything, ABE is a good reminder of this.

And ABE has not stopped reminding us!

The Now

ABE says we have become a triad – ABE, NM, and myself. It does seem to make for a good 'flowing' connection – and it's all about the flow. These days we are connecting for ABE communications almost on a daily basis. NM gets her 'nudges' (as she calls them) all the time. She sits down, receives and writes, then sends them over to me and I edit, format, and archive. Whenever questions arise, we also post them on the online document and NM goes online and posts her replies. The connection is now more fluid, informal, yet also stronger – or rather, deeper is a better expression. And this is now how our triad is functioning.

At ABE's suggestion, we have established a physical presence – a website – where random communications can be posted, and where ABE material can be freely shared. ABE likes to refer to this as our foundation. It's not quite that yet, although we hope whatever we are able to offer will provide some form of 'coming together' and sharing for the human family. You can find us at – www.thewaybackhome.one.

 Where are we going to go with this? We truly don't know – to be honest, neither of us thought we'd even get this far. Like all good, natural things, we're just going with the flow. And, of course, trying to remain in-synch.

I think I've said enough. I'm now going to step out of the way. That's it for now – read on.

KD

A Note on the ABE style

NM receives the ABE communications in a kind of 'stream of consciousness' style. That is, the words are almost entirely without punctuation and consist of continuous words rather than sentences. After I receive the communications, I read through them and do my best to format them into grammatical sentences. It appears that the sentence style can be somewhat 'archaic' at times. There are many 'but see,' 'but hear this,' 'see this,' and similar phrases. Actually, to be fair, these are very useful markers as they allow me to see where one sentence finishes and another one begins. There were times also when ABE seemed to say something in a way that was not the most fluid, or modern way, of putting forth. I wondered if ABE wanted for me to 'translate' their communications into a more flowing, informal manner. So, we asked ABE the following question:

> **In the formatting of this material we have made very minor adjustments, such as punctuation. We have not interfered or altered any of the wording. We wish to stay true to this material. There are some phrases that sound a little awkward. May we change these into better English, without altering the meaning or content?**

If you feel extremely strongly to do so then
yes. We would also like to say that if you are
on the borderline of wanting to, then we feel it
should be kept as it is. Love and Light - Abe .

There you have it — we were given permission to make alterations only if we felt 'extremely strongly' to do so. Otherwise, we were to leave it alone. Perhaps there was good reason for this. Maybe, just maybe, the transmission style of ABE is also impacting us as we read — acting upon our own inner cognition? I leave it to the reader to ponder more on this. For now, we've left it more or less exactly as it came forth — as it was allowed to be.

A Note on Book's Questions

Almost all of the questions that appear in this book are in their original chronological order of being asked. In this, nothing has been changed. None of the questions — or their respective answers — have been edited, amended, or in any way altered from their original context.

There are a few occasions where we received additional information on a subject that appeared at random — that is, not as part of a Q&A session but as a 'question-less' nudge that NM received. On these few occasions we placed these 'extra nudges' as running on from the answer to a related question. Yet overall, we would say that 95% of the questions in this book remain in their original positioning. That is why some questions may seem to jump about a bit in terms of their subject matter; or that we later return to an issue that came up in a previous question. The reader will do well to remember that many of these questions were formulated in advance of the scheduled Q&A sessions and so they naturally run-on without going back to clarify and answer. Some issues are thus returned to and clarified further in the text. Some of the questions may not be as clear as we would have liked them to be, in hindsight. Yet they reflect our own exploration as we tried to understand these experiences.

Rather than cut and paste these sessions we decided to leave them in their original format. You, the reader, are experiencing the ABE communications in virtually the identical way as we first did. And we would prefer to leave it that way. And from this you can find your own responses, and perhaps conclusions. Everything you read here is exactly how it came to us – isn't that good to know?

FOREWORD

There is no doubt that the premise of this book will challenge many readers. Yet the fact that you have this book in your hands suggests that initial steps have already been made. We say 'challenging' for the very notion that this book exists at all is contrary to the dominant, or rather status quo, thinking of our times. We are stepping on broken glass when entering the domain where religion, god, spirituality, and such matters dwell. We may be venturing where 'angels fear to tread,' as the well-known saying goes - yet if there are angels, then they are surely on our side. As the reader will soon find out, the way back home is a positive path – a nurturing way back to ourselves through the distortions and distractions of the modern world. It is no less than a homecoming.

Now, let us return to the issue of the dominant thinking of our times. The accepted 'belief' is generally (and we use this term loosely) stuck between 'there is an almighty god – and take your pick of the contenders' or 'life is an accident – it's a bummer but get used to it.' Like all things in life, this is a stark polarity. Yet it seems things are beginning to change, and the cracks in this rigid structure are showing through. In the West we are now beginning to understand, outside of religious terminology, the concept of the absolute one Reality. Science is now confirming what mystics and sages have said for centuries. The quantum sciences have validated that there exists an underlying quantum field – sometimes referred to as the quantum vacuum, plenum, matrix, or even the akashic field. From this underlying collective field manifests all materiality (matter-reality). That is, all material existence is fundamentally and inextricably interconnected - we are all connected to the same underlying field. Further, that this underlying 'quantum' field is not only energetic but also conscious. Not everyone agrees on this point yet. However, a number of scientists have now agreed that the underlying energetic field of all existence is pure consciousness.

According to the ancient Vedic understanding - All is Brahman. There is nothing that is not Brahman, for outside Brahman nothing exists – because all is Brahman – the ancient. As the Indian sage Sri Aurobindo once put it, in answer to a question – 'Brahman, sir, is the name given by Indian philosophy since the beginning of time to the one Reality, eternal and infinite, which is the Self, the Divine, the All, the more than All…In fact, sir, you are Brahman.' In this understanding, there is no separation between that which we may call 'god' on the one hand, and all manifestation and creation on the other.

The idea of a deity somewhere 'above' us, seated on a throne, and observing all that has been created, is the product of a primitive mind. As Abe would say, everything other than 'That' is part of the splintered mind.

So – why shouldn't we, physical-spiritful beings that we are, be able to communicate with the source of our manifestation from which we came? Is that so crazy after all? Earlier formulations may have framed this interrelation in terms of the 'far-away god(s)' – now, we can understand this as a communion between, to use a trusted metaphor, the ocean and the wave.

With this in mind, we suggest that the reader considers the following communications in this book as a conversation between ourselves. In fact, we did pose this as a question to ABE - **If our consciousnesses are intertwined, then is it possible that you know our questions before we ask them? It is like having a conversation between ourselves?** To which ABE replied:

> One could say that yes, for that is how we
> would see it. Like the whole universe is mad,
> talking to oneself…the whole universe
> talking to itself to be able to know itself.
> These things set in motion as little pointers
> to wake you up like alarm clocks dotted all
> about the universe.

So – dear reader – let us venture forth without our blinkers, our rigid belief systems, our socially instilled opinions. Just for the moment, for the duration of reading this book, let's just drop all this baggage and just allow – allow the conversations to take you to new places. You may never be the same again…

1ˢᵗ SERIES

–

SETTING THE SCENE

1.   Hello Abe. Can you explain 'who' is Abe?

We came forth as a collective of energetic form, but we very much understand that form is not classed in which your worldly physical reality is, so let us explain. I am Abe, I speak for many for in this plane of existence - separation is not of essence. We are a multitude of which is not ever born into the world of physical form as you know it; but understand, we are very much still a part. Take it like this - you are experiencing the world in your physical form in that you have a body; this body is not separate from the whole. You are of a denser vibration in which resonates to that of your home in which you are a part of. You are in physical form which means that you are energy, like us, but stood still as a point of attraction. You are part of what is all motion, ever-changing, but you are stagnant just for a short time. What we are, and I cannot come up with anything else that will enable us to speak of an individual consciousness, for it does not exist here, and it will not exist for you when this time is over. What we are is what you are, and life is never apart just taking form moving through and out of form, like a candle that burns down to liquid because it has changed its physical form - does it really mean that the candle is all gone? We are able to be an 'I' for the essence of communication; to be able to come forth in such a way that will enable us to convey that which is important. That your life here is of beauty and difference and separation; but here it is of collectiveness and oneness, free from conception. What we want to come forth to do is unify the two essences together to enable a humanity of divine essence, of divine being - to realise that in which you are and that in which you can become. We want to guide you to the way back home, here and now. Love and Light - Abe

2.   How would you describe your location in terms of place or space?

See, we are able to have space and time and place because of you. Like an antenna that picks up radio waves, they are never positionally located until a device is enabling it to be transformed. Our point of place is here at this moment but not of location at all. What is enabling us to come through is that the mind is expanding as you evolve. This will be so, as to let in more and more. What we want to do too is to enable this transition - to know of it but to also help guide so that it will not be of confusion. As to what is happening, we feel that at this time there is an epidemic as people are struggling. You see, like we say, you are stagnant, and you cling to this in your form. Energy is shifting you along and coming in to help flow, but like a dog with a bone you will not let go. Love and Light – Abe.

3.   Do you experience time? Does the concept of time have meaning for you?

Time is not a place, a point, it is really a social construct. It will never be able to be rid of as this is your human structure. From the very first part of human activity you have tried to ensure and predict and prove that 'I am here,' and time says so. This is really the essence of time - to locate and divide and direct one thing; to slice it up into little sections. But if you think right now, you will see that time is false - for when can you ever trace back? It is only memory, and it is so that it is happening right here and that too of your future. Knowledge that this is so then enables you to use time as it is and not how your existence has taught it to be. Love and Light - Abe

4.   Would you describe yourselves as a collective
        consciousness that perceives as a unity? Does this
        mean you gain experience collectively?

Yes, we are a collective consciousness. A web of consciousness, one could say, in which through all of time and space and place experience is woven in inter-relational, interconnected, and picked up as to what you are attuned to.

For you have your eco-systems right down to the very energy at source - your bodily eco-system, your environmental eco-system, and the cosmic eco-system all different levels, perceptions, points of place working in perfect harmony at each and every level but non-separated at all. Our connection would be that knowledge of what you are is lost. Our connection is to enable you to see this interconnection, this vastness of perceptual experience; that there is a wholeness in this separation and that which looks like discourse at one level is harmony at another. Love and Light - Abe

Let us come forth as to what true knowledge is. Philosophers all throughout time have depicted and try to understand what knowledge is. True knowledge from our standpoint is allowing that in which you are. All knowledge is knowable, it is just that you think that it has to be attained - every experience, everything, every flap of a wing, crush of a rock, birth of a child, cry of a death, are all a vibration, a part of a pattern intrinsically interwoven into a web of consciousness. All is known, everything that we know is what you know. There is no separation in this; this is really what we want to come forth to do. Take, for example, technology; it has allowed you to communicate all over the world. What you have within you is much more expansive. Each and every one is a part of this cosmic consciousness. It really is so; it is just that life has caused so many to be fixated on the known physical essence of your being and forgotten that pool of consciousness that is readily available to each and every one. When you understand this then you have knowledge. It was always there, our only advantage point to you is that we do not have the dense energy in which you call body. Love and Light – Abe.

5.   How can people develop their understanding of
        these vibrational levels and their harmony?

You ask about the levels in which the harmony works between each and all levels. Put it like this, it is vibrationally inter-relational like the body with its environment. Although they are not apart from it, it correlates, it speaks vibrationally to one another. You have just found this out through the study of trees and its communicational pathways. Everything is talking to one another whether known or not. When unknown, your vibrational essence can be hard and cruel, acting upon all that is around. Even if you do not utter a word, one could say that this web is an ever-expanding web of consciousness created by vibrational essence. Harmony is only sought between these seemingly polarities when all are connected, for if the heart was cut off from the body it would not function. As so with the whole of life -communication is of essence and with correct knowledge of what that actually means is of essence. We are not to say that it should be acted upon. No, quite the contrary - harmony is not something sought out, but something allowed and opened up to. Love and Light - Abe

Our feelings towards humanity is always one of great love - for how can you not love part of that in which you are, for that would defeat all that we are? We are not here to say that we are above and beyond, like many would like to be thought of - but we are a part of that in which you are and in which everything is. We want to show you this - to be open to the beauty of contraction and expansion. With Love and Light – Abe.

6.   Has any part of the Abe collective had
        experience of the physical realm of existence?

Yes, all have. Like we say, this field, this pool of collectiveness is forever dipping in and out of form. Religion tries very hard to describe this as Karma. Karma would be action, like there was something that acted. But what we say is a constant becoming; we are not of body, we are not of what your mind may conceive us to be. Therefore, it is very hard to put in words this consciousness is of one but also of many. Love and Light – Abe.

7.   Can you elaborate upon what types of physical existence has been experienced by the Abe collective? On this planet we call home and/or other planets?

Understanding of these levels is about vibrational alignment. To that of which you want to understand you can only ever move to that of the mechanism, the brain. To understand would be to evolve, but to evolve you must first understand that you are so much more than your physical essence. That is but the starting point. For energy to experience physicality it has to have a point of attraction. This point of attraction is but the construction of the mechanism; through time things have evolved. Every planet is different; every planet is vibrationally aligned with that in which it harbours. Like we say, it is inter-relational. If you are asking if there are different life forms on different planets, then we would be inclined to say that it is abundant all over the cosmos; but is a vibrational match - that is why you cannot see it. It is not recognizable in your form to be able to see. But as you evolve you will too see that the whole cosmos is alive. Love and Light – Abe.

All of life, all forms, for we can only say this because we have no form; to have no form is to be all forms and although we construct ourselves as a collective, we are a collective of all consciousness - all times, all space. This is the fundamental key - that all you are and what you will ever be comes back to this. You may not have NM or KD as you do so now, but there will be an impression of that for you too in this form or should we say as none for there will always be an essence of you. You are but the same. Love and Light – Abe.

8.   Is there a part of the essence or consciousness of NM and KD within the Abe collective?

But of course. There is no separation at all. It is so inadvertently intertwined we are surprised that there is even a construct that could perceive separation at all.

It is all about vibrational alignment. But see this, we are zero-point now. You see, all over the cosmos life is evolving at different rates. Your planet is fifth in evolvement; there are four more planets that are above your stages and many more below. We are not here to hurry your species along in any way, shape, or form - but to assist in the energies that are being felt. We have been to Earth many times before and have been mistaken for aliens or spirit, but we are neither. We are what you are evolving to - but also that in which you also came from. Now to answer that in which we communicate to others, we only do so to assist, never to direct, but to broaden the scope.

As to the stage of what the species are at, there are always people that are susceptible to subtle energies, although some are very much constricted to their physical life, but some are not, and it is easy to convey with such ones. As for the word intelligence, we would say that it is really been over-humanised, for intelligence is the way in which you collaborate and harmonise with your environment. It really is not something to gain but to be relational to. Therefore, if that is so the case, then it would be relevant to say that we communicate on all that can vibrationally align. This is done so by allowing flow without the stagnant self in human form, but not so in all other forms as this is not an issue. NM is vibrationally aligned because that signature in which you hold onto all day long is dropped. One could say that it is a falling into rather than a trying to align to. Love and Light – Abe.

9.   When you use the term 'vibrational signature' are you referring to the human mind/personality – or self – that gives the vibration a particular manifestation?

It is so. It is like the paper filter - a dissolvable one, but when it is no longer in resonance with the body, becomes whole again. But hear this, your laughs, your smiles, and love resonate within others. With much Love and Light – Abe.

10.   You said that Abe has been to Earth
       many times before and have been
       mistaken for aliens or spirit. How did this
       occur if Abe is a zero-state field – did a
       part of Abe manifest in form?

It was never as the form of Abe, you see, but of a filtering of consciousness of which the organism is resonating at. You see, it is allowed through you and will inspire and come forth in such a way, even if somewhat constricted by the brain's conditioning. Is this of understanding? You see, this is but more unlimited. In a way, we have been able to come through previously and this is because of evolution of the brain and the neural pathways. But see this, when there are so many pathways it will come back to but one. With Love and Light – Abe.

11.   You say that our planet 'is fifth in evolvement,
       there are four more planets that are above your
       stages' – are you referring to this solar system?
       Can you expand on this?

Good morning. It is well and good to keep this flow of communication. Now to answer the questions in which you ask. We would like to say that we are talking about five in the whole of the cosmos - you being the only one in this solar system. Now we are not talking as that to be of our stage because this would be within a zero-state and would not be of physical matter. What we are talking of is actual species that are in physical form and are at different stages of evolutionary process. Four more species are of more developed capacities of that of your own. In this it is a harmonisation of balancing energies. This is more so on a cosmic level, and why it is so that energy waves have been felt and people have been shifting and feeling these more intensely. As planets are in harmonisation and would mean that everything that inhabits it so indeed has to harmonise with it if they are to continue. Love and Light – Abe.

12.   Can you name these other four planets in the cosmos
         that are at advanced stage of evolution?

The planets are xylllion, kyoto, paledion and sylatio.

13.   Is our evolution somehow linked together? That is,
         we need to harmonize   our energies so if there is
         disruption here on Earth it will affect the evolution
         of the other planets?

The whole cosmos is interrelated and harmony within this system is of importance, but it is not led in the way you think - and destruction to you may seem like harmony to others, for your planet is always morphing to the energies available. See that human conditioning is so to be seen of doing and acting, and although there is need for this there is also a time to be guided by that. Many people are resonating below that of what the planet is resonating at, and therefore out of harmony. Then there are others who are resonating highly but maybe are not of the world. For your own evolution it would be wise to marry the earthly energies to be in sync with that first and foremost and to connect also with the cosmic consciousness. This is your evolutionary path at present. This would then harmonise the planet and that of the cosmos too.

14.   Are there other species not of the Earth who are here in physicality in order to resonate highly to assist evolution on this planet?

No, it is but a calling of this one thing. You see, it may have been necessary before because you were not developed enough so would have come through a secondary source. But now there is no need for this as you are evolving. Is this of understanding now?

15.   Are the planets xylllion, kyoto, paledion and sylatio known to us by a different name? Are we aware of their presence or location?

These planets are of this name and are located far from your solar systems, not even in your field of discovery; well, not at present. The species of these planets could well communicate with you in the future once the mechanisms to receive are able to do so - whether that to be of technological advances or of your own human body evolvements to receive such. The reason you can dip into this cosmic consciousness is because you are very much a part of it, but when in physical form you are entitled to block this out completely like changing the channel. You cannot hold and hear two stations at the same time, but in the future with your bodies changing to receive more and more energies then this would be possible of other species. Remember this, where we are coming from is a place of zero-state; also, your body is limited to the energies it can receive which is a good thing. At present, to go from one state to another without progression would be detrimental. It cannot be that way. Love and Light – Abe.

16.   You state that our present evolutionary path is to connect with the earthly energies. How can we best achieve this?

Yes, it is very much so needed to be able to align yourselves to this. Firstly, many have lost touch with their environment and, like the lizard whose receptor was covered up in an experiment, you are lost and out of sync with your environment. And when this is so, you are not functioning well. You are sick, out of balance, for to take the environment away from any species you see that their health deteriorates. So, it is of utmost importance to start resonating again to your home vibration. This is done so by that inter-connectedness, of being in nature and of bringing nature back into the system. It seems that in your earthly existence things have become very much sterile, and although may be seen as good has wiped important things out that allows this relationship between home and self. Realise this - there is never a separation and what has been taught is that there is so, and in this creating a great dissonance - correlation not segregation. Love and Light – Abe.

17.   You also state that we are morphing to the
        energies available. Is this how evolution occurs on
        this planet - by adjusting to shifting available
        energies? If so, what is the origin of these
        energies? Many people feel we are currently
        experiencing a transition upon this planet is this
        connected to a shift in 'available'
        energies? Can you explain? Thank you.

The energies are available from all around the cosmos. The original state is the zero-state: the zero-state is this endless becoming of form and of no form. Life is cyclic. Evolution is very much a vibrational process but also a material one too. See it like this, a human is physical in time and space; vibration is not only felt it is transformed to that of the environment. It is so very tightly interwoven that it is hard to see a starting point within your physical existence. It is correlation and transference that allows evolution in physical form, but it is very dependent upon the energies available to it. See a toaster - the toaster is working all well and good when the mechanism is capable of transferring the available energy to be of use to something within the environment. Higher energy for the mechanism will blow the fuse and be of no good; too little and it will also not be in sync to do what it has to do. Do you see? There is a transition, and like we say, it has to be a process rather than a jump. To get to the home resonance is important, but the next step is evolving to be more holistic. In that being the cosmos, we understand that it is very much in action as we see such energy rooted in so many. But even so, the social construct in which you are within is making it difficult to enable these things to flourish, and we realise there will always be a struggle to create the new. But it is turning, and it is a process. Like we say, we are not here to spread dire news, but for people who are not exposed to this kind of information to see and connect to something that has long been forgotten and is engrained in the wholeness of your being. Love and Light – Abe.

Energies, vibration, is always available to those who are open to it. These energies are also from this state of zero, manifested into physical form because of resonance. Some people can indeed tune into other vibrations that are seemingly not present to that of the masses. See, it is their own vibrational signature that determines the syncing up of vibration. A relativity of such, for relativity in the sense is a vibration syncing up or a system, a mechanism, that is able to receive such a vibration - one could say, more universal. Love and Light – Abe.

18.   You state the importance of connecting and being in balance with Nature. Yet our governments are pushing toward further urbanization and persuading people to live in cities. Isn't this contrary to the direction we need to go in? Could this be a deliberate policy to create further disharmony upon the planet?

Of course, this is so. Maybe not so intentional, although we understand some is; but lost in the ways in which have been deep rooted for so long. People, and not just governments, do not want to lose control - never understanding that they never once had it anyway. What is damaging to your home is only damaging to oneself, and most people are just not harmonised at all. In this de-harmonisation you can do nothing but spread that too. Love and Light – Abe.

19.   You state that we are at a time where we need to be guided. Are there other intelligences guiding our evolution upon this planet or working to assist us? Could you explain more on this? Thank you.

We are happy to be connecting today. We would like to communicate firstly that yes, we are in touch with other intelligences but see it like this, we are also not separated from them either. You are very much at a young stage in evolution compared to others, so we would say that we are not communicative with so many of your species. With other species around the cosmos this is not so as they know that indeed this separation from what we are and what they are is not definitive in no way shape or form, and in this we don't come forth in the same way as what we would to you. See, life is very singular, and we come forth to you in individual form or collectiveness to communicate and get across that in which you really do know. Sometimes you need to just wake up and remember that is our purpose. Love and Light – Abe.

20.   Is there a reason why you are communicating
        with us?

The reason is that you will bring these messages forth in a way that haven't been before. Your hearts are very much aligned and opened for this receiving. Not many are so in this way. In your non-egotistical open heartedness, you can receive and that is what is happening here - a clear channel, a clear heart. Love and Light – Abe.

The reason to communicate with you is because of again resonance. What we also would like to say is that the time is right, and people are all evolving at different rates for that is the beauty of life in all its colours and diversity. What we would also like to say is that indeed we do communicate with others but see it like this - if you are aware of this kind of thing, as we know that others have come before as to convey messages of love and light, you will understand that the message is loud and clear and consistent. And that is of unity, of collective collaboration; maybe not in body form but of a singular consciousness, one source. There are levels of consciousness; see it like this, to be that of a Russian doll - the further in you get the smaller and smaller the space. This is so with consciousness. Love and Light – Abe.

21.	So, you communicate to other intelligences -
	including ourselves - through vibrational
	alignment? Would you refer to this as a form of
	thought transference, or telepathy? Is this the
	fundamental form of communication in
	the cosmos?

Ahh telepathy, a heightened subject within your realm of existence. It is but the communication of the cosmos. But see this, it is not something that you are anticipating; no, but something in which you are to allow to open up to. See, this form of communication is not something that you are making your way to but to a way in which to remember as to that in which you have always held. You have long shut out things in which are part of your being of this world. You have many distractions and things to keep the mind occupied and stimulated but you are yet to understand the magnetic vibrational alignment form the core, the heart. Vibrational alignment is, and always has been, an open heart; for when this is closed off, you are not able to fully communicate. You have long been lost in language. I remind you of the saying, a good old heart-to-heart. This is it - this is resonance, this is truth. Love and Light – Abe.

      You say that the way of communication of the cosmos is a way we need to remember. This suggests we have fallen into a collective state of forgetfulness, or detachment? How can we move back into a state of alignment or resonance?

Yes, your planet is but in a slumber of sorts. The way to move back into alignment is to connect with each other, with the planet, with oneself. See, it has come about that relationships are dire in all aspects of life - with your beautiful home, with yourselves. There is nothing but judgement and condemning of feelings and emotions, like it is unnatural to feel. And that one should toughen-up and get on with it; make something of yourself, and the relationships to each other to be that of competition. Not many show their true selves, their true feelings, through fear of the heart being broken. That they must defend it at all costs - but it is not true. The more open your heart is the more authentic your life is, and the easy life can move through you; and in this not being continually offended by others. Love and Light – Abe.

23.   Do you have any relationship or attitude toward our species, humanity?

For isn't all just one relationship? We will say that again we are not separate, so for us not to feel deeply for your species and that of your planet would be shutting a part out of which we are - then who would we be to be allowed to speak of unity if we are so splintered too? Our position is that of unified consciousness, and although it seems to be that we are from another realm and something apart, this is really not so. The relationship we have is unity and for guidance from us - to be able to receive comes from your own splintered mind, it is not of our separation but of yours. When this is so you see yourselves as acting upon the world or the world acting upon you. It is not - it is a collaboration of consciousness filtered down through smaller and smaller, tighter and tighter, constructs. To see the wholeness is to really be in collaboration and to be in collaboration is to be in harmony. Love and Light – Abe.

24.   You suggest that we should 'open our hearts' and be more trusting in our emotions. Yet we live at a time of great emotional manipulation and exploitation, especially through our media. Is there a danger of becoming emotionally unstable or vulnerable if we move into our heart space?

For wouldn't it be the best time to do so when such things look so dire? Yes, people give you reason to not trust, but in the very closing down of your heart space do you not then close off to all that you are and all that you are to be? For one to be open-hearted could be said to be one of a selfish act, for you are the one that will feel life openly and honestly, therefore experiencing it in a way that is meant to be. We are not saying that you should be passive at all; an open heart is guiding and

if you truly are open then you will receive much more from life.
Is it not that what it is all about? Love and Light – Abe.

25.   Since there is no separation between us,
         as you   suggest, then in communicating
         with Abe humanity is actually in conversation with
         another aspect of tself? Is this the same as being in
         contact with our 'higher selves' as told in mystic
         traditions?

You see, the higher self has too been very much
conceptualised, and even though it is an aspect of you it has
been taught to be a place to aspire to in most traditions - that
this 'higher self' is meant to be of highness, as suggested in the
name, but is not as so. One could say an aspect of that in which
you are but also an aspect to that of which we are. In
communication with Abe you are indeed in communication
with self. We like this very much; we want you to understand
that there is so much division in your realm and we use 'realm'
lightly, and match this up to the analogy of the Russian doll as
we would not want you to misinterpret that there is some place
OTHER. Love and Light – Abe.

26.   Have you communicated with Earth or
        humanity on previous occasions? Have
        we known you by a different name in the
        past?

We are always in communication with the whole of the cosmos; it is just dependable upon what is open to receive, and at what the mechanism can allow. See it like this, we have conveyed with other beings, they have conveyed with your planet through others that are open to their guidance. It is an interwoven, interconnecting, vibrational web of communication. Love and Light – Abe.

All the knowledge of the cosmos is available like a symphony, an inter-weaving of existence. Our relationship is but the same as your relationship in that it is an interaction of seemingly opposites in a world of unity. For to discover anything of your planet, like greats who have come forth and dove into this pool of knowledge before, it has to be interpreted into form. These greats of humanity did but one thing and they tapped into this, into us; they stopped trying and just allowed. You see it as when you write - if you are thinking how to do so your writing can become entangled. To truly write is to allow what wants to come forth at this present tense. Love and Light – Abe.

27.   Is the Abe collective synonymous with Source? Has
         humanity in the past had contact with Abe and
         interpreted this as God?

Yes, is the only answer we can convey here. It was of a time of
very much a singular polarity mindset in which was captured
and overtaken for mass suppression of that in which you are.
We feel that it should not be interpreted as God, or source, as
these words are but too much over-used and overburdened
and really get in the way of that in which is truth. Love and Light
– Abe.

28.   It may be difficult for some people to accept that
         the origin of life, and of religion - the Source of
         everything - is a zero-state field. We might get a
         few blank faces! Would Abe like to comment?

There will be people who are not of resonance to this, of
course, and who may stare at you with a very much blank
expression. But hear this, as the pathways are built in those who
are of resonance, they are making the vibrational connections.
Then the pathways will start to be built too in physical form and
in physical form people will see and in this will allow these to
be built internally. Is this of understanding now?

29.	How would you prefer to express this
	concept we have as God or Source?

We would like to convey it as unity, or unification, to be a better word - the unification of self. Too long you have been splintered and divided. This is how things are now seen in your physical realities and have caused great pain to the masses, not only on your planet but to that of the whole cosmos. Love and Light – Abe.

30.	How has this caused 'great pain' to the whole of
	the cosmos - could you please clarify?

Of the de-harmonisation and destruction waving out as a ripple throughout all of time and space.

31.	Is this why there has been much activity to
	communicate with humanity in order for us as a
	species to find re-alignment and resonance?

Yes. We are here to guide and for you to see the unity in your existence and to connect you back up to that in which has be long lost. Love and Light – Abe.

We would also like to add that although there are cosmic repercussions from such disconnection it really needs to start at the base, and that is unification to one's self. There can never be anything universally accomplished from a splintered mind. Love and Light – Abe.

32.   There are wisdom traditions that teach a 'spiritual science' - a path of inner development - that may include certain exercises and visualizations. How does this path correlate with what Abe is saying about connecting with the unity field?

We would like to say that it does not quite correlate in a way - that a different approach is needed now. For so much has been contaminated, like a Chinese whisper that has gone around the world far too many times and now does not correlate at all to the original words first spoken. You see, it has gotten lost in translation. But hear this, you see there are not some long drawn out notions of healing within a person; it is simply coming back, a coming back to this. You see, it is but so simple that you overlook it for you think it must be drawn out for all this contamination took but so long to accumulate. But it is not so - it is an almost unity 'oh yes' and you can see and keep picking yourself up and simply bring it all back in. Is this of understanding? You see, we do not want to say that these traditions have not been of use and could possibly help someone loosen the grip in which you hold so tightly to your splintered self. But see this, you make it as easy or hard - it is but your choice. Love and Light – Abe.

33.   In the past there have been communications with other 'collective intelligences.' Can you comment on these communications? Were they expressions of self that were intermediaries, transmitting information from Unity?

All is but an expression of this, yes. It is but one - and if you were to collect this information all in one place you would see that it very much interlinks with one another. The reason in which we have come forth, and have continued to do so, is to take it back to the bare bones, if you will. Your species are evolving; no doubt it is seen across your planet, people waking up from the suppressed states. You see, it has been an infection of mind in that it has been too overused the way bearers will be the ones who keep their hearts open when all others want to close them off and put them under lock and key. Love and Light – Abe.

34.   You say you have come forth. Should we interpret this to mean you have become more manifest at this time in order to assist in our understanding? Does this imply we are at a significant moment in our planetary evolution?

That is exactly as so. And this is why things can sound in contradiction, but they are really not. For something to come to form it has to be of no form first and foremost.

35.	Are there currently other minds on this
	planet receiving direct communication
	from Abe?

Not in this form, no; and not of present time.

36.	Why was the name 'Abe' chosen - for any
	significance?

Abe is significant as to what NM brought forth of her own being. Like we say, it is of collaboration; this was a fitting name to that of which you would say abbreviation in that we can be of contraction. Is this of understanding?

Abe was short for abbreviation: abbreviation meaning a term that is of something that is of contraction; shortened, lessened, meaning we are to put nothing into one thing as to shorten, to put a doll inside another doll.

37.	You said that you have never been born into
	physical form, and yet you also state that your
	'collectiveness is forever dipping in and out of
	form'. To us this ounds like a contradiction – could
	you clarify what you mean here?

Ahh good morning, a good question in which to start with. The contradiction you see is of course from your own standpoint and we see it as so that there is no separation. For whatever is form, we are of it - but we would never take the form as Abe

or of any of the collectiveness. We are not a form like we say;
more so a pinpoint, a point of attraction than a form. So, we
have never been into form, but our formlessness allows to be
in all form but not of it. Is this understandable?

38.   Understandably, from a human standpoint this is a
      difficult concept. If there are ways to clarify
      further, we would appreciate this. So, would a part
      of Abe dip into physical form, such as part of a
      species? Is this how universal manifestation
      operates?

We would like to use the analogy of the ocean and the wave, but
we see that this too has been used by many. We would not be
in physical form for we are specifically a point of attraction of
which is being channelled. Never of form but you see what we
are and what you are is not any different, so we are in form but
not of this form. We are eager to answer these questions, and
we thank you for your continued connection. We do feel so
that this communication can move on quickly now. Love and
Light – Abe

39.   By being in material, or dense form, is life in service
      to the unified zero-state? What   can be
      understood by the concept of 'service'?

We would not like it to be one of service, for you see you would
be putting yourselves in a form of hierarchy of consciousness.

It is but differing stages and differing views. You see, if there was one big crash of a drum and that was that, it would be but an awful waste for you wouldn't have time to dance, for the moment you would of stood, the song would of been but finished. Is this of understanding?

40.   There is a phrase we like. It says – 'Simplicity is more complicated than it looks.' The truth of our connection to Unity is simple, yet we have complicate these matters. What would Abe say to this?

Like just discussed, the constriction of self is always up to you. You can resist and hold tight to that of which you know and feel comfortable with to continue - or you can allow much more. Is this of understanding? You see, simple is always hard for you in human form. For you see, that if it is simple and comes easy then it is of no importance. You know that this is not true at all, for life should flow. You clearly need to participate in this life, but life does not have to be battled with, just met. Love and Light – Abe.

41.   For millennia, humanity has talked about spirituality and the spirit. We have long searched for spiritual understanding. Is spirituality as simple as connection to the unity zero-field and allowing pure consciousness?

We would like you to see not as but a connection in a sense that you have to get up, plug in, and be of doing - but rather an allowance of. For if you are having to connect up in some sense, then you have simply lost the notion of it all together. It is but an allowance of it - to breathe, settle down, and allow. Is this of understanding of how spirituality is? For we would like to say that you are already spiritual, for you have just forgotten about your vibratory essence and connection to all. It is really a remembrance. It is but an understanding of what your heart already feels and picks up. Do you see? LOVE and LIGHT – Abe.

42.   So, the big question (and we have to ask it!) - what 'is' the meaning of life? What are we here for?

For the whole meaning of life is to live, and to live one must be allowing of all that you are. For to not understand that you are but of physical content but also of vibrational too, you are but living a half-hearted existence. But we think you have gotten the notion of this, so we will put it like so: meaning of life is you. There is no particular meaning that all of life should abide by. But hear this, meaning in life does so get lost when one is very splintered, for it feels like the whole world has taken a piece of you and you are but lost within the noise outside of yourselves. You see, we would not want to wipe the whole world clean, void of expression, for the meaning of life - if it is to be of anything - is this EXPRESSION of but one thing. For you see, there would never be a dance of life if one had to do it all alone. With Love and Light – Abe.

2nd SERIES

—

MIND, BODY & SPIRIT

1.   We often use the term 'God', yet this is misleading.
        What is your understanding of 'Divine Source'?

Ahh yes, God - the word that has caused so much hatred in your world when all was to be seen was the complete opposite. You see, we have come forth for this reason; because we do so indeed see that like we said, things need to be stripped back to the bare bones and this is so with your understanding of the divine and also of God. People are of course free to choose in that of which they do wish so, but for the ones who are not drawn to any of these terms, and we do so feel there to be many now, we want to say that God, Divine, universe, source, are all but one thing and you are it. Love and Light – Abe.

2.   Have earthly religions been successful in
        representing the Unification/Source?

We see that they have, and we are not saying that they have not served a purpose at a different stage of your evolution. What we are saying is that to move forward now these outdated ideas are not going to serve you well to see the whole picture. They are not so much to be rid of or dismissed, you would not say to your mother 'oh well, you gave birth to me a long time ago, you are of no use now,' for we are in a large cycle in which some point you will come back to the beginning and this will be the forever becoming. There is truth in all religion, but it seems that these things are driving humanity in the complete opposite direction to that of which it was intended to do so. This source or collective or God is that in which you are - how could it be any other? You have been sleeping and it is time to wake up to that in which you are, which everything is. We know that a lot of new age movements are saying that we are all one and this is true unification, but we feel that they miss it out that this is also science; it is also God; it is also every terminology that could be ever thought of. You can never dismiss others, and people will always have their own beliefs - but what we want you to see, to truly see, and not just that but feel - in the core essence of your being - that even in this world of great polarity I see you in me and me so in that. Love and Light – Abe.

3.	To return to Source - is this what you mean by *the way back home*? Could you clarify what you mean by this term?

The way back home is really first and foremost back to the home vibration - being your planet - and to be aligned with that, for we feel it to be too much of a step to go from low to resonating high with the planet. This step cannot be skipped; what we also say is that to do so you have to unify. Within a split consciousness of 'me and the world' is never going to be able to see to it that you are a transactional vibratory essence that is not separated from your world - more so, an expression of it. This is not to say that you do not impress upon the world either, for you alter vibration by that at which you resonate - so it is always transactional. So, to be unified it would be to see and wholeheartedly feel that you are transactional, that you are whole. Love and Light – Abe.

4.   How would you regard humanity's current spiritual state? Has our species had higher knowledge previously that was lost to us?

There have always been stages at which your species have been higher developed spiritually, but still it has been tainted by something outside of yourselves, that being of a God. The state of your own planet's spiritual evolution is progressing rapidly and has been so. That is why you see more and more destruction because of the fighting to keep the old. What we would like to say that there does not have to be a choice, just a knowing. A wholehearted feeling that what we are stating is truth - not because we say it to be but that you feel it deep in the core of you and resonates with you on all levels. Love and Light – Abe.

5.   You have said previously that the state of our own planet's spiritual evolution is progressing rapidly. Does that imply that the planet is a conscious organism? Is the Earth also in communication with Abe? Could you clarify this?

Good morning both. We are delighted to clarify but a few things, and feel it is of importance to do so. You see, it is so - but one could say that also the Earth and all differing planets are of a constricted consciousness. By that, of its own vibrational signature and to that that is upon it and also around it. You see, like we say about the pathways - within and also it is also so without. You have your connectors within the brain that create neural pathways due to vibrational resonance and this is so with your Earth. Now hear this, as your planet evolves and morphs and changes it will resonate differently and like your internal self will also create differing pathways too. Is this of understanding now?

6.   There have been many 'wisdom traditions' operating upon this planet. Did   they have access to Source, to the Truth?   Did you have direct contact with any of them?

Like we say, it would not of been of the Abe form; but we do believe that people have had this connection even unknowingly so. For some people, they are inclined to have this type of brain functioning in which they never lose this connection albeit how hard they try to shut it out throughout their lives. And there are others whom through evolutionary processes seem to have developed a masking of this connection and the brain develops differently. But this is not to be said that it is not available to them. One could compare it to, say, more so of a deeper sleep. Love and Light – Abe.

7.	There have been many spiritual Masters upon our planet. Were these ordinary people who gained access to the Unification energy, or a deliberate material manifestation of consciousness?

But of course, we would like to tell you that all who have ever walked your planet have had this connection to unification energy. But also, too, it would be a deliberate material manifestation of consciousness because it would have come forth in such a way as this. Love and Light – Abe.

8.	Are there other terms that have been used/are in use that may help to clarify the Abe state?

The one who has come closest would be that of Zen tradition; and we understand that you have to name things in your world of polarities. Zen too, in a way, has become tainted for it is seen as people taking themselves apart from the world which it is not - but this is now tied to the word Zen and people see it that they would have to give up all that they love. The only way is to be of it and in it; there is no truth up on the hilltops but here in the midst of it all, in the polarities of existence, knowing that it is all quite ordinary but seemingly extraordinary all at the same time. Love and Light – Abe.

9.   Is true science a knowledge of vibration? If so, will
we arrive at this knowledge?

We feel that indeed science is a knowledge of this vibration. But it can never be truth in the sense they can measure and record with seemingly pinpoint accuracy. But it is always going to have to compare things and always have polarity. In this you will find marvellous ways to be in your world; advancements and knowledge of it. We are never to dismiss this for it is who you are too. You are human beings of your world, but it will have to always measure and dice and slice and in that will not have the full picture. What we see though would be something of a merging. If science can see the completeness and the undivided essence of life within their boxing things up, truly see it - and we are sure it is already going in such a way - then that would be of essence. Love and Light – Abe.

10.   Is vibration at the core of our health? How can we
heal ourselves with the knowledge of vibration?

Vibration is a core essence of health care, for vibration is the language of life. For you to be out of vibrational alignment of your very own being, if you are split, then you are creating discourse within the body. Everything has a vibrational signature, so it is true with that in which you put into your body for that is what tells the body what the outside world is like - if it is thriving or not. So, it has to be of great importance that you are 1) aware of the vibrations of the things you put into your body and 2) that of your own vibrational signature. You see, this too is inter-relational. You could have all the best food and eat well and exercise but if your own vibrational essence is that of lack that you are eating this nutritious food, then you are no better off than eating all the junk in the world. For you see, there are people who are extremely fit in the world and have health problems because they are not aligned with their own vibration and that in which they are putting into their bodies. Is this of understanding?

11.   Is certain healing knowledge being deliberately
        withheld from us? If so, why is this?

I think it would be of both. See it like this, there are people on your planet who know of these things and are keeping them alive within their communities. Indigenous people pass this down through the ages by ways of ritual. What has been done, that more so in the west, life has been pushed in such a way that this knowledge is seen as new age or mystical, that logical reasoning and science can be the only way. What we would like to say is that there is also a dissonance in this and if unified with the so-called mystical and that of science then medication will be a thing of the past. But you see, your very system has been built on such grounds now and will be difficult to re-establish without a fight of someone wanting to hold on to some sort of past. You see, it is never about one better than the other but about the merging of both - the unification in things. Love and Light – Abe.

12.   What will be the future of human health?
        Will our health systems be forced to change?

The future of health really does lie in the people's way of change for they too need to shift and let go of past habits that do not serve them. You see, you know in yourselves and your bodies when something is off, if you are attuned to your being, and you would know how to nurture your body back to equilibrium. But we are not saying that you need to be dismissing that which is of your physical world, and science, reason and logic, for they are intertwined aspects of who you are and how you experience life as a human being. It is in the emergence of both that the key to health really lies - but we feel that both sides will find it hard to let go of their deep-seated beliefs at first. But it will happen. Love and Light – Abe.

13.   What will be the future evolution of the human
        body?

The future evolution of the body will not be of the body but be that more so on the consciousness level. Not so much on the physical to start with but as the consciousness of your being rises, or one should say resonates, the body has to adjust too to the higher vibration in which way the body will not be so dense, it will not be so heavy. Love and Light – Abe.

14.   Is this evolution of the body to a lighter
         form a natural evolution that occurs in all
         dense matter as it develops? Has this bodily
         evolution occurred before on this planet? On
         other planets?

It is a natural progression for they would not be in resonance. But see this, for you to become and be of this world there has to be some kind of density that is also resonance to that of your home Earth. This would be subject to all species and you will then see that really you do resonate on a physical level. It can be no other way. See, what we have now is what many people speak of as the love vibration that being of the cosmos, and this is true in a way. We want you to see that there is an expansion coming, evolutionary, that will enable your species to expand in consciousness to that in which we are. But hear this, it will always be of a density to match that of your planet. It can be no other way, and this is so with others. Love and Light – Abe.

15.   As the human body becomes less dense to
         resonate with an altered consciousness, then how
         will this relate to the physicality of the planet and
         other species upon it? Will there be a similar
         shift in their density too?

Yes, it will. But see this, they will be subtle changes over time and never a leap as you see it has always been so, and will always be, of harmonisation to all that is of the planet too. Is this of understanding? It is always inter-relational, and you will not be of such lightness or transparency with that of your planet Earth for it is rather dense in its vibrational essence, albeit shifting. Love and Light – Abe.

16.   How do you mean we 'will not be of such lightness or transparency with that of your planet Earth for it is rather dense' - will humans not be 'of the earth' in this time, or that the Earth will not shift in the same way as human bodies?

No, you will but shift to that of the planet for you cannot outgrow it at present. For the purpose of conscious evolution, at this time, is to put deep roots into your planet. Is this of understanding? But hear this, for if the planet is making other connections and is not at all of resonance to that of its beings, then they will grow increasingly uncomfortable upon it. Do you see this?

17.   What is the importance of food and diet for human health and awareness? Can you say something about the current state of our food systems?

It is important in the way that it is inter-relational to that of your own vibration. Like a sock in the wash that is dominant in colour, it will colour all that is mingled within it. So, it is important. Like we say, it allows the body to sense what the outside world is like - a vibrational communication system. The current state is that it has been far way taken from its own harmonious balance to that of the Earth. To see that your Earth is suffering is to see that you yourselves are also suffering. You are creating a dissonance of vibrational communication through the toxins and chemicals that are being used at present and, in this, creating a cognitive dissonance. Love and Light – Abe.

18.   Does a contaminated vibrational signature affect the food we eat and vice versa?

Always it does - it is but transactional. See it like this, someone who but knows no other than being that of their own vibrational signature are quite dominant in a sense to get their point across. Someone who may be not so caught up in it are not so and are seen as introverted or shy. But hear this, they are but allowing – see, it has been the dominant that has been cheered on for so long but in this you have gotten too caught up in this game. And we may have strayed again, but you see the dominant force lords it over and therefore whatever is not allowing to meet and be of benefit to the system is not going to be one of health or of nourishment. Is this of understanding?

19.	What is consciousness? How does this function with the human body/mind?

Consciousness is the signature of form but also that in which it comes from. It is this. See this again with the analogy of the Russian dolls - there is consciousness, then there is the doll. This is form. Then there is another doll - another form. And inside that, another doll, until you come back around and there is consciousness again — space, emptiness, one could say. Although space nor emptiness is ever void. You see, consciousness is always at a point of attraction to that of the mechanism, or should I say organism. To be pure consciousness is to be void of form completely. See, we have no form; therefore, we can be everywhere within all form but not of it. This is hard for your brain to conceive for it is always working within the parameters of polarity. It is about the essence, the knowing of this form, and allowing consciousness to have a more fluid flow. Is this understandable?

We would also like to add that mind is not consciousness - it is your unique vibrational essence.

20.	Our histories, our experiences, etc – do these help to develop each particular aspect of consciousness? When each vibrational essence, or consciousness, returns to no-form (Abe) does it retain any sense of individuality within the collective?

This is but a fine line. See it like this, a toaster which has the electricity running through it but when thrown away or broken beyond repair it is unplugged. You see, there is no obvious notion that it left or imprinted the electricity upon this one thing. But hear this, like we have mentioned before, it is a joining up for the evolution is not of just you, no, but that of the whole cosmos. To answer more direct, there is not a specific part of you that is in the shape of you. But you see, there is but a web of consciousness - to be one of connection not of form at all. But you see, it is a vibrational pattern that can be tapped into, almost like a membrane. Is this of understanding? But please, do hear this - it is never of two separate things, just a filtering through as such. Love and Light – Abe.

21.   Our minds – or vibrational signature – also reflects our personalities. Could you clarify the relationship between consciousness and our individual selves?

It is but a filter, in a sense. But see this, it is not two distinct things - but we do so feel that we have to explain as such in your world of polarity. It is but always in and of itself, despite the separateness you do so feel at times. It is a change of vibration in which to bring into form that of which you resonate of. Is this of understanding now?

22.   How is consciousness linked to evolution upon our
        planet and within the human species?

Consciousness is what we are. See, we are only a point of attraction; because of the brain this then creates the vibrational signature you see as mind. Mind is not a part of consciousness; it is a part of that which is body. It is the unseen signature, your vibrational signature, that speaks in vibrational terms and resonates. Consciousness is devoid of form - it is zero point. Mind is not consciousness but your vibrational language back to consciousness. Is this understandable?

When mind is dropped, when you do not cling to that of your vibrational signature or self, pure consciousness is allowed to flow.

23.   So human ego is blocking the flow of pure
        consciousness? Does this suggest that we should
        detach from our personalities in order to allow
        connection with pure consciousness?

You can never but detach, it's about meeting in the middle - in the knowing of it as unification, never a one or the other. But hear this, it may be of a good notion to but put it down and see - to rest without trying to uphold it as you do. Love and Light – Abe.

24.   And how would this flow of consciousness
        be linked to human evolution? Is it also somehow
        linked to the evolution of this planet? That is, can
        we participate consciously with our planet's
        evolution?

Yes, that is so. In the allowing of consciousness to flow you are allowing life to move. We know you hear this now as more of a Buddhist view, but what we want to say is that consciousness should flow - yes, but you should also be able to unite matter with this. This is where your evolutionary key is - there is no way at all that this energy will not be influenced in some vibrational way in your existence. It cannot be so, this is life - but in the allowance of it, it will really propel you forward as a species. Realise this though, we do not want any species to be void - for what would be the point of that? Love and Light – Abe.

25.   How would you suggest for humans to develop
        their minds? Are there any specific practices, such
        as meditation?

Meditation is great but sometimes can get caught up with escaping here to be in your body. To be feeling all this, to be a part of all there is, and also to be able to know the expansive truth too whilst here in physical matter – wow, what an experience. What a life. Be with it, feel it from the centre of your being, and most importantly – participate. Love and Light – Abe.

     It is said that the human being has an organ of perception that can be further developed. Some traditions say this is necessary for our evolution as a species. Can you comment on this?

This is to be so of the pineal gland. There was an experiment a while ago which we may of mentioned previously, about a reptile that had this sensory organ connected to perception covered up and struggled to read it's environment. What we would like to say is that it had been of importance in a way. See it as this, you are a blind man of the world and you realise that driving may be off of the agenda. You still are able to sense the world with your stick or dog. See, the dog becomes an extension of your sensory apparatus, enabling to help you navigate the world. But if you had your eyes back you would not need this. This pineal gland has been beneficial in the past, when your brains were not so developed, but are not necessary for the way the brain is developing now. Just like everything else, the vibrations enable life to be pieced together and harmoniously intertwined in a way that you could never imagine. Love and Light – Abe.

We would like to say and end today by saying that you are all in control of your own each and individual evolutionary signature. That is being human, and in life sometimes it causes you to be bitter and resentful and closed off from this web of vibrational communication that is now being spun right from the very first thread. It will always be contained within consciousness and therefore the more united it becomes the more this vibrational essence of each and everything harmonises. The more available it is to you - all vibrational alignment - this web of communication will infinitely expand. With Love and Light – Abe.

27.   You have said that some people's brains develop differently, and so block out their natural connections. Has social conditioning within some of our cultures been a deliberate attempt to wire human brains in such a way as to keep people in slumber, so to speak?

This is indeed so. For like we said before, how would they be able to sell your parts back to you if they do not firstly recondition and break it apart in the first place? For you see, it is a game of life in which you have been coaxed into playing, and in this you have thought that it is indeed what life is all about. But this is not true, there is so much more to it. It is just that the wiring is all wrong - you see this? You also have to remember your parts in it too, for you have been hypnotized by the highs of modern-day society and when coming back to this it all seems rather dull, rather un-special. But you will see that the one who is awake will indeed see the extraordinary within the ordinary. We know that this is not included within the question, but we would see for it to fit. You see, the DEPRESSION epidemic is one of dissonance because people feel torn between vibrational alignment and the rewiring of the vibrational alignments of the brain. In this you see that now too depression can be a false premise to keep you in this game also, for it will be nurtured and hung around in far too long. Is this of understanding, as we know that we may have strayed considerably? With Love and Light – Abe.

28.   Thank you, Abe. Yes, this is important. If social
           conditioning is a deliberate attempt to keep
           people unaware, or in slumber, then is it because
           there are those in power who understand the truth
           - the truth of what is Abe and of our connection to
           Unity-Source? Or is it only because slumbering
           minds are easier for   social management and
           control?

It is so that people are to use this power in a way to manipulate, and it is also so that people are set - they are not at all interested in getting out of their seats for they have all that they need right here, do they not? Why question it? For you have enough food, even if it is not right for you and the system, but that doesn't matter for you have the little pill to fix it too and in this a great dissonance and a great disservice to all that you are. For some will go an entire lifetime and have never lived a single true moment in their entire life. What a shame. What a waste. With Love and Light – Abe.

Ahh, good morning. We see that this is of importance here to convey. Love is a vibration felt by the heart and directed and labelled by the mind or vibrational signature. You see, all vibrations are felt; they are then filtered through mind or vibrational signature. Your own unique vibrational signature transforms a vibration into a thing. As it is transmuted by it, it is transformed so then that love vibration which was felt, say between people, was pure consciousness flowing but you labelled it and made it a point of attraction or pinned it upon a certain person or thing. You see, the vibrational signature holds it all. See it like this, you start off with a large lump of clay - we will call it unity or unification or consciousness - you then want to play and make separate things, holding it to account with experience. These are the vibrational signatures, what we would like to say is to realise it may seem like different things, but it is still just one thing - that being clay. What we would also like to say is that it is not a bad thing to love people, and we know in your world that love is very conditioned, where love in reality is unconditioned. It flows - feel it but don't direct it; don't mould the clay and tie it to things and people. Love and Light – Abe.

30.   But what about our world of relationships?

We see that this can be confusing for you would say if we love all in a way that no-one gets special treatment, that you do not have close intimate relationships, then you will be destined to be alone. But we do realise that you have a circle in which you are in close proximity. We would never say to not love them in a way that you do - but to know that what you love in them can be extended to a stranger on the other side of the planet and not have to be so contained. It does not have to say that you should love everyone in a way you love your husband or child, but to see that there is no difference in the love that you feel on the transference of it. See, the more you have open-hearted communication and connection with others you realise that you can do nothing but love them. Love and Light – Abe.

31.   Why do I not love others and then feel stronger for
         another?

You see that your vibrational signature can cut this off through past experience. This love is in constant flow, constant motion, when the heart is open; but as we say, your vibrational signature wants to open and close and transfers it, filters it through past experience in a way as to protect the organism. You see a person, you have all the vibrational conditions, and you either allow it or block it. You then match these 'now feelings' to that person or place or thing, which in reality was only a memory or a belief and like we say, you let it flow or you allow. Love and Light – Abe.

We would like to add that you see that some people give their love freely to others and some do not. It is all about that vibrational signature. You see, when you first fall in love you are forming this connection. It is allowing universal energy to flow between you, unrestricted, because you do not yet have any conditions of this love, this connection. As time goes on, you experience more of life together and you bank things in the vibrational signature bank. It gets cluttered and love is not able to flow; it gets stuck within these patterns transferred. What we would like to add is that you can love without possession and love without conditions - you just have to see that. Love and Light – Abe.

32.   You discuss love and consciousness as vibrations, and about inter-relationality of all humans. Yet how can we make this knowledge 'real' for people? How can this information help people to live better lives? What can we do?

First and foremost, it is of importance to be human - that is it and that is what we would like to get across. Humans have flaws and accepting them is a way to resonate higher. See, what people think of your so-called 'enlightened ones' is that they have reached a different place, and it is not true at all. The gurus know this; this is why you see so many Buddhist monks smiling, for they see this simplicity of being and how much people struggle because they think that they have to be somewhere higher, that this is not enough. What we say is that it is all here and only the splintered mind cannot see. We would never see to it that you drop your vibrational signature, and we fully understand that this is so ingrained in your experience. What you can really see is that you are not it - you are a long track of vibrations and matter and endless cycles of life and form. In that seeing, in that very knowing, how can one really be splintered? How can one honestly say that they are me and you are you? It cannot be so, and when this is seen as clear as day then, well, you will feel no need to be anywhere other than here, basking in life's undivided beauty. You will do nothing but radiate love and connection for it is all within and therefore will be all around. Love and Light – Abe.

33.   Have humans distorted the love energy/ vibration in our physical existence? How should it be used? Have human civilizations made use of it differently at other times?

You must see that all vibration is distorted in some way or another in your physical existence - it can be no other way. Like a light that hits an object and bounces off in other directions, it is so with vibration. Now see this, though your own vibrational signature is but built with many differing vibrations, resonating to make one like water that passes through a sieve - whole, separated and whole again, this is so. The pure stream of consciousness flows through the body, through the brain, and is transformed by its conditioned state, by the vibrations that it holds, it is interlinked and also attached to: it is your vibrational signature. We understand that this seems like all individual things, but it is not so. What we are really trying to say is yes, the vibration is always changed by our own vibrational signature. What we are saying is, if you can allow it to flow - and this is done by allowing universal flow - in a way of direct experience of life. See it like this, to have the pure water you would not need a filter; it would not help. The filter may have contaminants that may affect the water which is already pure and in this being more a hindrance. So why not drop the filter, allow pure consciousness to flow by cutting out the unnecessary middleman. This does not mean to be pushed around and passive, but to have direct experience with life. Feel it, be in it, open up your hearts to allow its love. See, in your human form there have, and will always be, people who try to manipulate this energy flow in a way for self-preservation. But it cannot be done for if it is open heartedly flowing, then you are having direct experience with life. You see, the patterns and the self is there but a part of this whole. The only people that know of this, and want to manipulate this, are the ones who push for self-preservation. Love and Light – Abe.

34.   You have stated that Abe is 'zero point.' Does this
        mean that the Abe collective consciousness is the
        prime energy that is the source of all things? Is Abe
        where all physical consciousness manifests from
        and returns to? Is there anything 'beyond' Abe?

This is so, that we are where all form is and where all form is
born from and will eventually fall back too. There is nothing
beyond this because there is nothing. For in the nothing you
hold everything; it is within the spaces of things that you really
have life for. You see this within all your music and language
- if there were no space there would be no life. Love and Light
– Abe.

35.   We all share the same consciousness - we are Abe
        and Abe is us. We are aspects of Abe in material -
        or dense vibratory - formation. Is this correct?

That is correct, and we like to keep going back to the Russian
doll analogy for it shows that you, and only you, restrict this
flow by means of being engrained and engrossed by the
vibrational signature. Hypnotized by all its goings on, treading
carefully as not to offend or hurt this vibrational essence; but
in the seeing that it is just this it can be let up. Love and Light
– Abe.

36.   If our consciousnesses are intertwined, then is it
         possible that you know our questions before we
         ask them? It is like having a conversation between
         ourselves?

One could say that yes, for that is how we would see it. Like the whole universe is mad, talking to oneself. But you see, you also do have this vibrational signature for a reason too - for that being there can be a myriad of expressions of just one thing. How wonderful that is to see - we do not say get rid of this but rather allow more in by letting it up. You have become so frightened by it in a way, and in the knowing that it is not really what I am; and 'I am' is a lot more expansive and inclusive. You can realise that life isn't so terrifying, but a great expression of one thing and you can go ahead and just live, just participate. Love and Light – Abe.

37.   Is all human thinking a process of receiving/
         tapping into this collective consciousness? Is this
         what is meant by inspiration – what the Greeks
         called the Muses?

It is so, for when you open up the doll you allow space to flow. It is not another within another but believe us when we say that you are opening up the dolls and are not putting them back together. People are letting up on this vibration - but only fear keeps you restricted, for in the fear of loss of self that you will not exist. This has been a vibration from the beginning of time that humans want to say that 'I were here' and that 'I existed' and here is the proof because 'I am me,' but what they do not see is that it is a false identity and if they just let this go a little they will see that there is so much more to be open to, so much more to be receiving. Love and Light – Abe.

38.   When artists such as writers or inventors receive their ideas, are they transmitting ideas from the collective consciousness field? If so, is it not the case that ideas have been seeded through such channels to help to evolve human civilization?

These are great questions and we feel that there need not to be such drawn out answers from us for we see that you are of great understanding for you are very allowing of this flow. For in your own work you have but help open minds and create foundations for evolutionary steps forward. We have a question to you - how does one feel when writing of these things? Do you feel yourself, or that you are allowing something other? With Love and Light – Abe.

39.   As an example, popular science-fiction books and films are sometimes used to manifest and distribute ideas for later possible actualization?

This is true, for sometimes it is great to get a message across by a song or a film or a book for this widens the scope to which people are touched by these things. See it like this, as in the previous question, the whole universe talking to itself to be able to know itself. These things set in motion as little pointers to wake you up like alarm clocks dotted all about the universe. Love and Light – Abe.

40.   How does this relate to Carl Jung's theory of the collective unconscious?

Very well - for was he not just doing the same and bringing this universal consciousness into being through his own vibrational signature, and in this he let up on his own vibrational signature to allow that of the one consciousness to flow? Love and Light – Abe.

41.   You have previously stated that 'there are others who are resonating highly but maybe are not of the world.' Could you clarify what you mean by this?

We would mean so in the term of not your world, and of the planets you are yet to discover. See, all is at differing evolutionary stages, and this is of harmony. Love and Light – Abe.

42.	Does Abe distinguish itself from other
communications that have been 'channelled'?

To us, we would feel like this is, and has been, of use to those whom seek that way. But for us, it is really of being human - we do not want to take you to our being for what would be the point? But it is more so of a seeing and realisation of how great and wonderful it really is to be in form. There have been so many that have tried to take you away from this by trying to reach a higher state. What we feel is that it now needs to be grounded and brought right back down to Earth for it really to be of any use to humanity. Love and Light – Abe.

43.	Many traditions talk about 'higher consciousness' –
what they really mean is a rise in the resonance of
one's vibrational signature? Is this rise coming
to everyone as part of natural evolution? Is there a
method whereby a person could individually
accelerate this vibrational shift?

Good morning, we are happy to have this continued connection with you both. Higher consciousness is indeed that way, not a higher place to get to but a resonance in which you are more accustomed to be - more open to receive. Now see here, we do not mean for a person to have to resonate at a certain point like you really have to do anything - it is of the notion of coming to grips with that in which you are. There is never anywhere to get to, just a knowing of that this is how it is. Now, if you are asking as to move this along more quickly, then it is really just in the allowance of this knowledge; really getting to realise and understand that this is how it is so - by truly experiencing it and done by allowing it to flow. Love and Light – Abe.

44.	What is the role of DNA within human evolution? Is it also a vibrational code? What is the function of the majority of unknown DNA once referred to as 'junk DNA?'

Ah yes, it does indeed make us laugh at the word junk for is it not in the knowing that something to be of use and is now not? Well, this is not so; it is just that your sciences indeed are not able at this point of your evolution to decode that at which they are not open to. You see, the more open you are to this flow, these vibrations, the more you let go of your very constricting conscious mind, you know that when you let up a little space, you allow something to move - and in this you are able to not only understand but clearly see. Your DNA is very much the vibrational code of life - it is vibrational memory. Like we discussed earlier, one big conversation going on but to itself. One could see it like this: you have your parent's vibrational signature and through this you create and wind these two seemingly different vibrations and create a new vibration. This is but the structure of your DNA. Love and Light – Abe.

45.   In our physical reality, right now, there are a lot of
           problems with obesity and food- related illnesses.
           There are also an unprecedented amount of
           chemicals in our food production. Are we creating
           greater dissonance with our bodies?

But of course, this is so, for you are trying to control and conquer something you do not have the whole picture of. For if you really could understand yourselves then you would indeed not want to put the things you do so into your bodies. The harmony of the body cannot leave out that of your environment in its natural state. For you are mixing up the vibrational alignment by trying to straighten it all. But you see, you do not need to do so for in the straightening out of a wiggly line you are flatlined. You kill it - do you see that this so makes sense?

46.   What can you say about the rise of genetically
           modified food sources? Some people consider
           them our future - should they be introduced into
           our food systems?

We see that there are many people on your planet - and believe that as this continues to grow there will be more of a need for growth in your food production. What you do not see is that by making these modifications to your food you are indeed making these modifications to your planet and in turn the cosmos - it is always inter-relational. There will always be ways in which life will cause you as a human species to modify life, to upgrade, to solve, and this is indeed good. But in the seemingly extreme concentration on one area you automatically denounce another. It needs to be more open and understanding of these vibrational essences of life and the inter-relational connection of everything. For if this is understood clearly you can do nothing but automatically move forward, and in this flourish. Love and Light – Abe.

47.   How important is physical exercise? Should we know our bodies better? Practices such as yoga are popular now – are these good ways to develop body alignment and resonance?

Mm, yes - see exercise as so an interaction of seemingly two separate things. You see, your ancestors moved all day long until it was time to not do so; and we know that advancement in technology has caused many to be very stagnant and still. A lot of times throughout the day in this you are not allowing this energy to flow; you are not connected, for when you are stagnant it is so that energy is stagnant. This actually slows down and lowers your vibrational signature. See this, though no movement is better than any other it is purely just movement needed, if your vibrational signature is matched to that. To do yoga - by all means do that. You will indeed get much from it, but if it is not so then it will be of no use VIBRATIONALLY. See, we discussed this resonance earlier with you, talking about food and then your being is begrudging of not having a different food. As such, it may well be good for the mechanics of the body, but the vibrational alignment will be out of whack. Health will never be healthy until you take on board that you are also very much a vibrational being. You can take care of the mechanics, but you also need to take care of your vibrational signature. This meaning, you also take on the vibrational signature of that in which you eat. We are not denouncing these great ways of getting people moving as they do indeed also make people aware of their own energy, etc. What we are saying, that no one is better than any other form of movement providing you are aware that you are also vibrational. Love and Light – Abe.

48.   Greater numbers of people are suffering from addictions, especially alcohol and drug related. How are these issues related with the times we are living in?

They are in a way to escape this - that you have been so tightly focused on self, and how and what you should be doing and being, that you look out on a world that is tough and disconnected and lonely. You see, all these things do, really, are allowing you to drop you in a way. You are not that, and many people know this, but society is saying you have to uphold this idea of 'you' or you will not survive. You will not succeed, and the dissonance is caused - and when dissonance is caused you want to escape this. It is so very sad but so true, and we are not saying that you should feel sorry for people who use drugs or alcohol, for there are many who do not so but are maybe obsessed with changing lovers or addicted to food or sex or working. See, anything can be an addiction in a sense, to escape this life. I suppose it is just what people are going to choose as their vice. Love and Light – Abe.

49.   Diseases such as cancer have increased
        dramatically in recent years. Why is this?

We can say but two words and that is - vibrational dissonance. We feel so very strongly to convey this at this time as we see it ravaging the body of many, taking countless lives. It always starts off as dissonance, always. Love and Light – Abe.

50.   There is a lack of understanding about death in
        our modern societies. It feels as if we need to see it
        as a transition stage rather than as the end. What
        are your comments on this?

See, death will always be so that it is hard to grasp, and of mourning for many who do not understand the part of that in which you are. Clearly, you have some emotional attachment to, say, of a dear friend or of a loved one. It will always be so, and you would need to let that vibrational part of you come up and express for there is never any sense in pushing it down. You do not need to become unattached to life. You see, in the beauty of that heartfelt release of another, you feel alive. That is beauty, that is part of being human. What we would like to say, that this is not the end. It is of the body as it cannot continue, but your vibrational signature is always in the mix, always. It is like making a cake: many ingredients make up one thing - a cake. That is what we can say as to life after death. You see, people saying that they have a near-death experience and they may well see a light, for the signature is still there; it is still running through, but it is still very much a human thing. When you have no body, you are no longer splintered - you are back to wholeness. That is it. Love and Light – Abe.

51.   Continuing the theme of understanding the end-of-life transition. Could you say something about the process that occurs after the death of the physical body?

The end of your body is not the end of life, just a change in form, for you always go back to the whole. What we really want you to see in your human form is that you are a cycle - that you are this wholeness. There is deep beauty in this process. There has been much fear around death, and it is understandable in a way as your mind works in the polarities of life. You see, this vibrational essence of who you are is a part of this wholeness. It is not soul; you do not leave the body - the body changes form. The vibrational signature that was once blank in a sense, or zero, is now going back to the pool of pure consciousness. Life is a process and there are always different stages. The vibrational signature does not leave, it just hasn't the bodily resonation to sustain it, for it to be stagnant, so it returns back to the source. But hear this, it does not become lost. It is a collection, but not of physicality. Like a soul - a wholeness in life or consciousness constantly expressing itself, constantly talking to itself. Does this explain it well?

52.   What can you say about the concept of reincarnation? Do particular vibrational signatures return to form to continue with life experiences?

One could say that you have all lived every life for it would be silly to say that wholeness or oneness has not lived all lives - so this is of truth. What we would like to say is that there are also resonation of the vibrational signature. You see, your religion is very much based upon a physical entity of sorts that would lord upon man to be good and moral, so religion imposed the idea of a cycle coming back and back until you finally get it right. There is some truth, in a sense, that life is cyclic - but no truth in that it is to get this life right. You see, that is very much a human concept; for if you are not thriving in this life, surely you could then be in the other world. But there is no other world, and to some this can be disheartening. There is just one world in different expressions, and that one world is the whole thing - the whole show, for it cannot be any other way. So, we wanted to express to you that if there was a matching of vibration, one would see this as the soul cycling around and around. But it is not the continuance of a person to another, for an essence of your passed ones is in the world, in everything. There are specific signatures that attract signatures of another type, but it is not of you going into another body neatly packaged to live again. It is not this way at all but essence. Some might think that with this information humans would be lost but it is not so, for you will fully see that all is of you, and that there is no definition. Love and Light – Abe.

53.	Why does vibrational consciousness come or 'birth' into form? Are we here to have specific lessons or experiences?

Life moves, life cycles, life is change and life is consciousness. We would like to say that although religion and society has taught you in a way that you are here for lessons or experiences, it is not this way. You see, the thing that you call soul does not have to reach a higher state for it to be accepted with open arms and to say 'good job.' No, the overall point of all of this, the whole point of us being here, is to wake you up to that of which you already are. You are an expression of one complete thing, so to say. That you are here for lessons would in some way say that you are not already what you are. Here is a little story: a baby kangaroo abandoned by his mother was taken in by a pack of hyenas. Now all was good and well until one day the grown kangaroo bumped into another kangaroo. The other kangaroo hopped off and the kangaroo was in awe of this creature. He went about trying to be like the kangaroo but could not be, until one day the hyenas came clean and he was told that he too was a kangaroo like the one he had seen and in that moment of knowing he was able to hop and jump just like the others. You see, it isn't about lessons - it is more so about remembrance, like connecting back up the phone line that you had left off the hook. Again so, you are connected to all that you are. You see, you always have everything you need - you just need to see that. Love and Light – Abe.

54.   Could you explain if there is a difference between what we call pure consciousness, soul, and spirit?

No, all but the one same thing - and we would be even reluctant to call it anything other than this zero-state. But do hear this, soul and spirit are that too of vibrational signature. But you see, that they are but one thing - albeit the row of identical flowers that each have their own scent. Is this of understanding?

55.   You have said that disease is a result of vibrational dissonance. Could you explain more on this?

Vibrational dissonance is when two vibrations are rejecting or repelling each other. They are not harmonizing; they are not attracting each other BUT also there are more dominant vibrations. Say, a heavier vibration, a denser vibration compared to something that is just okay. See this, when you walk into a room and there has been an argument - you feel the density in that room. You feel as though your whole being is weighted upon - this is the true meaning of dark energy. So, in regards to disease, dissonance is caused by two seemingly different vibrations trying to be held at the same time. Take it like this, you hate broccoli. You had a bad experience and was extremely sick when you were a child eating some. Now the doctor comes along and says that broccoli is the only thing that will make you better today. You have complete vibrational dissonance. See, life as you experience it, and in this your own vibrational signature, is being wound together. The body always wants to work in harmony, always, but it does that by vibration; by talking to each part vibrationally. This vibration is, and always needs to be, in resonance to that of which you are, and also that of your environment. But you see, it is not so. For example, you could eat something that is factory made, that is dead. In a way it is vibrationally talking to the cells, to communicate that in which your environment is like. In this, the vibrational signature will be lowered because it tells the cells to act in a certain way. But see this, if you are eating only organic food and your own internal vibration is not a match to this, this also creates dissonance. There was a lady whom only ate fresh organic fruits and vegetables, never smoked or drank, exercised regularly, and still died at the age of 35 from a heart attack. This was because her vibrational dissonance was caused by the vibrational signature she had due to her heartache. She was so focused on her health and wellbeing she forgotten about her relationships, and in this she felt that dissonance in her heart. Life is always about balance - always. Love and Light – Abe.

56.   You state that DNA is the vibrational code of life.
        Could you explain more about the role of DNA?
        Also, how does DNA relate with consciousness?
        Will human science come to work more with the
        properties of human DNA - and how?

DNA is the building blocks of life, it is true. For in this vibrational code you have all the knowledge of who you are. You see many new age groups saying that you can wake up your DNA for the codes for activation of higher consciousness, and this is true. But see this, it only carries what is up to now, and presuming that you are not fully evolved then you can see that there is point at which you will get right back to here. But see this, DNA is also a receiver of vibrational code, so you are creating new vibrational code by your own being. You contain vibrational code from that of which you have come and evolved from, but also you can receive new DNA structure by opening up to this one consciousness. As you see, this is evolution; this is the way in which your species allows itself to take the steps forward. Is this of understanding?

57.   You have said that humans can receive new DNA
        structure as part of their evolution. Is this similar to,
        say, receiving a new program 'update' that
        provides new information for developing? Could
        you say more on this?

It is in the creation of these pathways - so it is but put into the program to pass on a memory bank of evolution. Is this of understanding? For when new DNA is then created it is binding together what is two resonances and creating but one new – and, one could say and hopefully would be, improved, evolved. Hear this though, it is also a receiver of what is. Love and Light – Abe.

58.   You stated that 'many new age groups saying that you can wake up your DNA for the codes for activation of higher consciousness' and this is true - up to a point. Could you clarify more on this? Thank you.

It is true, in a way, that you can awaken that in which has been and what is already present. It is not true to awaken pure consciousness. You do not need to activate it but allow this vibration. In this, you see, it is moulding together past, present, and future ancestry vibration - your vibration and that of pure consciousness. Is this of understanding?

59.   In that case, is it really necessary to have New Age groups performing these rituals   like a service? Can we not allow this activation/flow ourselves through our own intention? Is there a personal method for this?

This is what we want you to see. It is a very human condition to put power outside of yourself. There really is no need for this - it is indeed through your own knowing. You really do have to start to pick up the pieces that have always set you apart and really start putting this cosmic puzzle back together to wholeness. We are in no way denouncing these practices for they do awaken people to be more open, but many get so caught up in it. Love and Light – Abe.

60.   Is DNA the code of life for the cosmos? If so, how does DNA function for other planets and other species?

You see also that DNA resonates and picks up your vibrational code. It's like a get together of past, present, and future, and then deciding what to build its foundations on. It is the code of life on all planets and works exactly the same for all species all over the cosmos. Love and Light – Abe.

61.   How did DNA originate? Was it 'developed' in some way?

DNA is but the code of life, the building blocks in physical form to pass on that at what stage you are but at. As you are moving into less of a physical evolution and more so of a conscious one, you will see that DNA is also a receiver of vibration enabling it to be built and to bring together that which resonates, an attraction of such. For from the very first building block was born but from the one thing, but enabled it to become split, and in this it was breaking down into smaller and smaller parts, marrying parts together through resonation. For the first whisper of life it was born into be that something of separation. But you see, it was not just an expression, a dance of life. Is this of understanding?

62.   In terms of bodily health, is it expected that human life spans are going to increase as part of our future evolution?

This will be so, for your life span is always increasing due to the technological advances and the more complex the brain becomes. You see, these vibrations create new neural pathways, new connections, and in this building a new structure. This means you will become more complex. Your bodies will not be so dense as the vibrational essence rises on your planet, and in this will allow the system to thrive for longer. But see this, technology will be a large part of your futures. You will have morphed in a way to be part machine and this will work, say, when you lose a limb or something dramatic happens to the body - it is of use then. What we would like to say is that in this vibrational evolution, this one of consciousness, it will be evident that you will live longer, for the body will not be so pressured - the vibrational signature will not be so dense. Love and Light – Abe.

63.   Human sexuality in terms of gender roles seems to
       be shifting, and blurring. Many people are finding
       that to be either 'male' or 'female' does not fit
       into their physical and psychological well-being. Is
       this related to our current evolutionary shifts?
       Could you comment on this?

Ahh, we see this and would like to say but one thing - social conditioning. For in the splitting of, say, more and more genders you are but casting the net of more separation. The people who do not classify that they are but one or the other are so just saying 'I am human, and love is love and this is it.' We see that things get lost - why not be that of being human? With Love and Light – Abe.

3rd SERIES

–

HUMAN SOCIETY & CULTURE

1.	What is your knowledge and perspective upon our history here on this planet?

But of course, every vibrational signature, every experience, has come back to this. But hear this, you know all that is - you are able to always tap into this knowledge by allowing it to flow by unification. We are not something outside of you. Take, for example, the Wizard of Oz, the great old wise wizard of Emerald City, knower of all. But honestly, when you pull back the veil, just a normal man. You only limit yourselves by shutting out that in which you are. For if it is not of substance then it does not exist. Tell us, what does it mean to you to exist?

If you are but asking us to reel off history, then we can say this - there has been great famine, destruction, cities found and lost, civilizations come and go, and this will be so again. Your planet, and the cosmos, are in constant flux - and the ones who resist and hold so tightly to what they believe, and cannot move forward with this, will surely not be able to keep their own heads above water due to the new vibrations, due to this new energy. We say 'new' in a sense of that it is new to your form right now. This is what has happened before, and it will surely continue. Love and Light – Abe.

          Thank you. You say we need to keep our head above water due to the new vibrations. What can you tell us about these 'new vibrations?' Are we going to experience a period of increased disruption?

We say new in a sense that it is new to your physical bodies of this time and space. We would like to say that these vibrations and energies are manifesting at great intensity and there will be ones that fight hand and tooth to keep things the way they are now. You see, when the seed is cracked open it could be seen as completely destructive, when in essence it is bringing new life. For the new life to come forth, the old shell that contained this new life will have to crack open and this will be extremely destructive. For the more this energy is brought forth, or we prefer 'allowed,' you are tapping it in and grounding it down into this reality. In this, it will shake away all that has been built, and in this you will see that the ones who cannot walk this path will not be able to succeed. Love and Light – Abe.

To answer if there is increased disruption, we would say yes - as there are many that are grounding this vibration. They are unifying this of us and that of you, so the more people do this the more it will be destructive for the systems in place now. When you see more disruption, you will know that more people are enabling unification. Love and Light – Abe.

3.	Are there ways in which people could better 'ground' this vibration and new energy? How can people consciously assist in allowing this energy vibration in?

The unification: by knowing what you are, not allowing too much baggage, too many human conditions. Our very work is to show you that you are it; that there is not a stagnant self that lords upon the world but a process of life - a united field of existence. If we can get this across to as many as possible; if they feel it in their very essence and truly deeply embody this truth, then wow - change will manifest in even the darkest of corners and it will light up all that is still hiding in the shadows. Love and Light – Abe.

4.	We would like to assist your work too. Please indicate to us how we can best do this. Is it good for us to continue with our questions - does this assist the process?

It does assist very well, as we feel these are very appropriate to the things that people will ask and want to know. And we feel that sometimes we denounce or dismiss - but this is from a place of pure love and not to be of 'I know' and 'you do not' for we state that all this is what you are. It is really to loosen the grips you have. And although you are very much loose in your grip, your mind gets lost in the language - in the naming and pinpointing of particular things. What we would like you to truly feel is this - tell us, what allows for your inspiration to flow, for you to feel connected?

5.　　　Some traditions have a cyclic understanding of development, such as the Vedic Yuga cycles. They say we pass from an Iron Age to a Golden Age. Could you comment on this understanding?

There will always be cycles, and we believe there are many names for this. With the one you state in your question we understand to be of an already established structure. We are not to denounce your structures and your beliefs but to loosen the grip. See, you get so very lost in language - naming this, making it stagnant, pinpointing, separating. Our basis is always unification. If this can fit into the idea that you have for unification, then it is of use. If not, dismiss it. Love and Light – Abe.

6.　　　Some theories state that planetary evolution occurs according to electromagnetic cycles, or other cosmic energy cycles. What can you say about this?

We will always state that this is true - but to what notion do you have of cycles? It is built upon structures of old that have so much baggage tied to them. For life is really cyclic - you know this. You are forever becoming but never getting to see things.

Never stop and start, just change, interact, morph, but never a specific time or place. Science does like to pinpoint a cause and effect. But you see, when you pinpoint one interaction you forget about the others that have led it to this, and then to the ones before. Does this answer this?

7.   What would be a more correct way to consider evolution upon this planet? How are humanity a part of this evolutionary   process?

We would say that evolution is always vibratory. We go back to the Russian doll analogy. For you to have your own planetary evolution, it has a knock-on effect to other places in the cosmos. And for their evolution it is also the same for you; it is so tightly inter-woven that to pinpoint this evolutionary process you would have to go right back to unification. And to see the end result, you would see also unification - and in this you can see the pattern of the forever becoming. Can you not?

8.   Can humans delay or interfere with the planet's evolution, or is it out of our hands? Current thinking says that we are disturbing evolution (climate change) or advancing it (geo-engineering). Yet isn't this hubris?

There is a very fine line to tread here. We would like to say yes, you can interfere, but not so much in a way of physical action. It needs to be of this conscious, this vibratory action. You see, there will be many who will denounce this knowledge just so that they can be active in the world - active being in the physical sense. And although we see a time to be in action, we also see the need to be from no action; for you to then take the correction from a place of truth - your truth. Love and Light – Abe.

9.   It has been said that for the past ten thousand
        years we have had the possibility for conscious
        evolution - that is, our species evolution can move
        ahead through deliberate, conscious, directed
        effort. Can you comment on this?

You see, to have something conscious, now you really have to 'allow.' Being conscious is the key to this unification. It is an allowing of pure consciousness to be present in this time-space reality. It is who you are. We don't expect you to slay your vibrational signature or dismiss it at all, for this is also the creative essence of consciousness. It is about bringing together the two. You see, your unconsciousness is your vibrational signature, and when you are not conscious it runs the show. But by being conscious, you allow these two to unify; not ridding of any one, just allowing what you are and what you think you are to exist in this time-space. But see this, they are never not flowing; but you can be unaware and lost in the unconscious, never knowing that there is so much more to your being. Does this answer the above?'

10.   So, what you are saying is that by allowing pure consciousness to flow through us and into our reality - onto the planet - we are assisting with the evolutionary process. We don't need to struggle to assist evolution. On the contrary, we should learn to allow it all to flow and to ground it? To use an analogy, the human species is like a vibratory, resonating membrane - or skin - for the planet?

You need to stop resisting evolution. Stating this is not how it is meant to look. You see, this theme is in much of your life. By allowing, you sync up with the knowing that your way is not necessarily the right way. Love and Light – Abe.

11.   So, what you are saying is that by allowing pure consciousness to flow through us and onto the planet we are assisting with the evolutionary process?

That is but so - you are but not distorting it so much. But see this, like light hitting any physical thing it will bounce off in all directions, expressing in different ways. This is so, but true of this too. Love and Light – Abe.

12.   As all planetary evolution is interwoven, would it
         not be disastrous for the cosmos if humans
         destroyed or greatly damaged the Earth, such
         through nuclear war?

Oh, but of course. For unification does not hold place for war. For in the unification knowledge, you understand that what you do is only but done upon you. Love and Light – Abe.

13.   The phenomenon of crop circles has intrigued
         many people. There is the hypothesis that these
         are messages being given to us to help our
         understanding. Could you comment on this
         phenomenon?

Ahh, the crop circles. Now see this, there have always been signals, interventions, for we live in a unified field of consciousness. There will always be pointers, and symbolism has been used throughout the whole cosmos. And although you may not understand it, it can be decoded. We would be more inclined to think that it has come from a human tapping into or being of this energy source, rather than a little green man flying in. You see, it takes a lot for other species to enter your dense atmosphere; and even more so, for they do not want to be seen to interfere physically as to impose or direct. Is this of understanding?

14.   Many areas of the planet are known as sacred
        sites or 'energy' sites - such as Stonehenge in the
        UK. Did our ancestors have specific knowledge of
        cosmic energy? Could you say more about
        Earth's energy sites or energy lines?

There are such sites. But hear this, they are no more sacred than your back yard. You can tap into this anywhere. There was in your earlier conscious evolution specific points, and only because they built up the intention to connect in a certain spot did it become a portal or a place to connect. You see, if what we are saying is true - that all is unified - then how can it not be here and there and wherever you go?

15.   You say that such sacred sites are no more sacred
        than our back yard. This is good to know. Yet what
        about certain energetic 'hot spots' – such as
        sacred buildings (Alhambra, meditation halls or
        tekkias) – that are said to connect and facilitate
        energy flow. Are these places not more conducive
        to the flow of pure consciousness?

No, they are not at all. They may have this sense that they are, so people are to believe that it is so and therefore build up intention of it being so. It can be felt because of the people and the resonance of connection, not because of the place. Love and Light – Abe.

16. What can you say about energy lines that crisscross the planet? Some of these are well-known and may be pilgrim routes. Others are said to connect specific places. Are these not like planetary neural connections?

Like we said, it could be so likened to that, yes. They are of but conscious communication talking of and to itself - vibrational resonance, a membrane as such. Is this of understanding?

17. Have other intelligences, or species, been involved with assisting the evolution of this planet? If so, in what ways? Has there been knowing human collaboration with other intelligences? Why is this subject so taboo in our societies?

It is so taboo, for you do not understand yourselves. It would be spoken of if you could so get to a place whereas you knew all that you are. For in the knowing of oneself, you are knowing that of which you are. If you know this, then you can see that it is all a part of you, and it would not have so much fear. For humans think that they have to impose their way - only because they are not consciously aware. But do you honestly think that other species that are more evolved think in this way? It is not so. If you are asking if other species have assisted, it has only been when people have opened up to this, an intention if you will. Love and Light – Abe.

18.   Developed societies have entered an accelerated phase of materialism and consumption. This is stimulated by corporate greed. Is this a sign of our old systems and will this pass? Did other civilizations also pass through a phase of intense materialism?

Your existence, like we say, is one of cyclic motion. It is but an outdated system of consumerism; but understand, it will never be completely rid of it for even in the waking up to this there will always be a form of consumption in human nature. You are right to say that it has been completely monopolized by some that are based in greed. But this too is balancing itself. Your job is to be awake and conscious of it. Now there have always been civilizations that have taken too much, and in this, resources dwindle. What happens is that the Earth will bring it back to balance. Really, all you need to be is aware - the planet knows its own balance like you do with your own body, if you are aware. We would like to add that yes, humans find a resource and they take it and they see that it is beneficial and in this it is monetized. And although this is not true for how other civilizations conducted their affairs, it is still in some sense of truth. But you see, it does balance itself back out when people awaken and connect. Love and Light – Abe.

19.   The population on the planet has accelerated
        dramatically within the last century. We will reach
        9 or 10 billion people by 2050. There are some fears
        of over-population. Is this accelerated population
        part of our current development? Some people
        are worried about this. What is your perspective?

Over-population is always of keen interest. Look at it like this, if the soil is fertile you would have a good crop. You need space between these crops so they are able to truly flourish, to be able to maximise the growth of the plant. You see, when over-population occurs, the space is clearly getting smaller; your cities are built higher and your countryside is expanded and land is taken to accommodate more people. We always come back to it, but balance is key - and people to resources is of essence. When you upset this balance by, like you say, over-population you are putting these crops closer together. You are manufacturing foods that are not built for consumption. Everything becomes quick and more, and in this a great dissonance is served. It really is a knock-on effect, a cycle, and you are it. We would also like to state that as lifespans of humans expands this will also cause problems in regards to your population. You see, with this kind of problem there is no obvious solution other than restrictions in place formed by society. But we would like to say but one thing - this new energy that is upon your civilization has to resonate to that of the system. If not, you will not be able to go forward in this physical existence. This is all we would like to say on this for now. Love and Light – Abe.

20.   Our political systems are largely corrupt, and
        people are losing their trust and respect in them.
        We are due for a dramatic change. Is this part of
        the necessary transformation required upon
        this planet at this time?

It is. As more and more people awaken, they will see that indeed things are not in balance, are off - like you have been so conditioned in a way. As more and more people come back round, in a sense, they will see. But see this, people will be outraged and disappointed and angry, like they have been betrayed and hypnotized and befooled - and you will see all this mayhem and pushing back. You know, we like to say that you can never fight the old by fighting it. You are keeping it there in prominent position. What does the person who wants to force their way always want? It is a reaction, a resistance, an argument - but that will not solve the matter. We really want you to claim all yourselves back before you can take a step forwards to action - this is our purpose and it is also yours. Love and Light – Abe.

21.   The global finance system seems to be a
        manipulated and 'rigged' system that favours the
        specialist financial players. Yet the flow of money is
        also an important system of energetic exchange.
        What can you say about this?

It is an important energetic exchange and has always been so, albeit in many different forms over time. We would say that this exchange is coming to an end of physical money as you know it. You will be going forward with a digital currency in which you can see firmly taking place and rooting as we speak. There will be people who claim more, and channel it in a way so that it benefits a few manipulating and directing this system. But you see, as more people get wise to this the more they can claim it back. You see, many coming together is a lot more powerful than the one holding the bunch of notes alone. They will not have power or place to manipulate if people unite. That is why they push to keep things splintered - people disconnected. A united nation is a powerful force. Love and Light – Abe.

<table>
<tr><td>22.</td><td>There is a lot of talk now about digital currency - it can be used for greater transparency as well as greater control. Will digital currency not just replace the old system and maintain the same inequalities and struggles?</td></tr>
</table>

Not if people are awake for it can be directed, in a sense, as to barter, to exchange goods for goods, not to accumulate and take stock of. It just will not be in the sense as what currency is now. It cannot continue this way. Love and Light – Abe.

Our whole stripping back to basics is for us an un-conditioning of what you have for so long seen yourselves to be. Because other humans have placed them upon you, it is time to, in a sense, break free from the hysteria and come back to oneself - if you are ever able to unite. Love and Light – Abe.

23.   There are many people who view that the world is really governed by a small group of elites who are holding on to their power. Can people really make a change through their individual efforts or consciousness?

Like we say, it is not something that can be fought. You see this with many things now. But hear this - people are waking up, but are also falling into another trap of consumerism and political disconnection, thinking that always they have to pick a side when there is no side to pick and all is worn out. Then you may see, but we are coming forth to hopefully make you see a lot sooner. For if left too late, everything else will have been completely exhausted. Love and Light – Abe.

24.   At this current time our societies are becoming more authoritarian and controlling – especially through technology. Are we moving more toward control societies? Will this not cause conflict with the free flow and expression of consciousness?

Someone who is not awake will always want to control, for if a person is truly awake, and we mean truly, they will feel no need for domination whatsoever. Now, to say if you are moving forward to a more controlled society, the answer could be - yes. But you see, in this suppression, this pressing something down, it will at some point have no other choice but to bounce back. Love and Light – Abe.

25.   Propaganda and forms of social conditioning
        seem to be very high and there are great efforts
        directed into this. At the same time, you speak
        about individual power within each of us. How
        do you view this situation?

You see, it is like this - a tug-of-war pushing and pulling, always trying to get the little knotted red line to the centre of the line. You see, we are not saying that life should be euphoric, and it should be likened to that of heaven. If there is a heaven then it is here with you now, and the same with hell. You see, you are human and there are interactions and individual vibrational signatures and much more. What we want you to see as clear as day is that in which you truly are. Truly take it all back, all those feelers that state you are this and you need that and on and on - such a tiresome existence. It is in the realization that 'oh I am here, and I am also that, but I can be this' - and share it. Isn't that an existence? Isn't that the true beauty of a human life? Society does indeed dumb you down and cut you into so many pieces for if it didn't so, then how would they be able to sell you your fragments back? Love and Light – Abe.

26.   You have stated that we need to realize that we
        are everything – we are 'it.' Yet is this really
        enough to create change within our societies? To
        know something does not always result in tangible
        internal transformation.

The transformation will only come when you realize this. For if you do not break such a constricted pattern of being, then how will you ever see any change? We are never saying to not act but acting from the same patterns are never going to create different results. There will never be change, and you see this in many of your worldly affairs. Love and Light – Abe.

27.   The majority of people upon this planet have not yet 'awakened' to the truth. They prefer to watch television, or play their games. Do you see this situation changing? Will the newer energies arriving on this planet create some dissonance here?

Yes, it will, for it is like there is something in the air - like a nice smell of, say, fresh baked bread and they see that 'oh I am in life again.' They start to feel and shake off the monotony of just being and start living. But see this, it is much easier to sit back down and numb-out again because people are so afraid to feel, to love, and to live. What a shame! If only they knew that, wow, this is what I can do - I feel hurt but in this I am alive, I am here, I am participating. Such beauty in this realization. Love and Light – Abe.

28.   Our technologies now connect us across the globe. We are communicating like never before. Would you say the Internet is a reflection of our own internal connectivity? How do you envision the development of the Internet?

It is a physical adaptation of that in which you are. It is showing you in physical form to unite, to communicate, to interact. The same as when the phone was invented - it had the same effect, bringing this energy that no-one could conceive at all and putting it into your physical existence for you to believe it and use it. Now, for people who are able to adapt to this new energy, or allowance, there will not be such a need for these physical technologies. It is some time off, but you as humans will be connecting and allowing this flow of communication. See this, the heart is the connector vibrationally and the head is the receiver - just like a phone line. If these are both open to receive then it will be that way. Love and Light – Abe.

29.   It seems that upon this planet humanity is evolving toward a planetary civilization. Is this so? Does this suggest we are moving toward a world government? Is this shift to greater centralization a part of the civilizing pattern, and has this occurred on other planets?

We would like to see this movement towards a united government, yes. But see this, we have said before that even you, as your own vibrational essence does not need to be rid of it, is truly, truly in the undoubtable knowing of unification. If this is so, then we would hope that there would be no need to be governments but just humans. It has happened on other planets; but you see, they are a different species and different formations and have resonated different from the start so have not conducted things the same. They too have made mistakes and are in no way superior, just more evolved. Love and Light – Abe.

30.   Human societies place many layers of social conditioning upon their citizens. People adopt belief systems, ideologies, etc. Are you saying it is necessary to de-condition ourselves, and if so, how might we go about this?

Good morning both - we are pleased to see this continued connection. Your human society is but built upon social conditioning. It really does take you further down the rabbit hole. Its outdated structure is just that – outdated. It does not, and will not, resonate with the new wave, the new vibration. This is why things can look destructive - for in the holding onto old outdated structures one tends to get aggravated and at dissonance. You see, this new vibration people are feeling like we said 'the winds of change' - but they are not sure what it is. This is where we would like to come in and lend a helping hand or more. So, both in physical form, this connection - these words - will resonate with many, for we wanted to get it down to the bare bones again - no nonsense. The way to de-condition is by needs of allowing this flow of energy. Allowing the heart to open and allowing the mind to be free. This will take work, for hearts have become closed, and also that of minds, which you know is your vibrational signature. Loosen the grip on the story of 'me' and try to allow the story of 'we' - of unity. Love and Light – Abe.

31.	Human civilization on this planet is currently at the
	phase of nation states and nation-blocks. Yet isn't
	this a limited stage that we need to supersede
	and isn't nationalism a limiting vibration-pattern?
	Could you comment on this?

But of course. It is as we said above, people feel this need to hang onto something, to grab a hold of their identity. Some tie it to their country, some to their football team. See, people live a lot in fear - in fear that people will take what they have: their status, their belongings, their identity. When they feel threatened in this way they fight back and want to claim what is rightfully theirs. See it like this, your media puts a spanner in the works; by the end of this the whole factory is shut down wanting to never see a spanner in their factory ever again! What they do not realize is that the spanner contributes, and it was put there in such a way as to cause aggravation and separation. Is this of understanding of what we try to put to you?

32.	There is a growing trend toward increased urban
	living – larger cities and more mega - cities. We
	feel that there should be a balance and more
	rural living. Is it not important to cultivate agrarian
	lifestyles and to live off the land?

See this, in an ideal world people would be more self-sufficient, cultivating the land and going off-grid. But you see, many people are not wanting to take this route. They like their cities and cafe's and hustle and bustle. What you can create though in these places are more natural spots, more open spaces: roof top farming, a box on the window, community projects, connection to each other and the world around. For this would be of great benefit, and you see people coming together again already doing such things. In the Second World War supplies were limited, people were taught to work their land again, cultivating what they have, growing what they could. This was forced upon people, and although we do not like the idea of directing we do feel that there will be a time in which this will be implemented again due to population spikes. Love and Light – Abe.

33.   Should more people consider living 'off-grid' – that is, more independent and sustainable lifestyles? Is this a good future direction despite it going contrary to current trends?

It would be, yes. But we would like to see it more community focused for it not only gives connection to your world but to each other - working together, cultivating together, sharing the food. For the best meal of the day is really the one shared with those you love, is it not? Love and Light – Abe.

34.   Despite our high levels of connectivity, more people are becoming strangers to their neighbours. Does not the sense of unification also apply to our human communities? Will current trends not also trigger a rise in alternative communities?

Yes, this is the way we see it going - for in unification you cannot but move into a more community focused setting. People would say that they would not feel good to be in a commune, but it will not exactly be like that. More so, a gathering of communities working together. You will see this far more so when your currency that you have now is no longer of use. You see, people think that in this sense of doing this you will be taking a step backwards. But it is not so. There will be deeper connection in this to your world, to each other, and also to that of your instinctual human nature. You cannot shut out that in which you are - and believe us when we say you have been running away from this truth for some time now, through fear of stagnation and no progression. But this also is a falsity. Love and Light — Abe.

35.   Heart communication is a strong vibration and creates harmonic resonance. What social or cultural activities would help to promote this harmonic resonance?

Connection — open-hearted connection - this is only implemented when you drop the vibrational signature, the conditioning. See it like a heavy bag that disallows you to open your arms and embrace life. For when you put it down, not get rid but stop trying to uphold it, you feel your arms free to embrace life and each other. This is the way of the open heart and this is when true connections are made. Love and Light – Abe.

36.   Are sporting activities a form of developing teamwork and harmonic resonance? Has sport been used on this planet as a channel, or vehicle, for promoting higher vibrations amongst our species?

It is in a way, yes. Team work is important, but you see it is still quite limiting in a sense that even though society has built teams it still separates by way of stating my team is better than your team - and in that sense you are not better off at all. The idea is one of a global team, and although it sounds euphoric it is not. The one cause that all can be working towards and what you all share is humanity. Love and Light – Abe.

37.   Our cultures promote values of competition, conquest, and control. We sense that we need our vibrational influence to shift to values of collaboration, communication, and compassion. Will these values be more dominant in our younger and upcoming generations?

Yes, but of course. They are born into this vibration. It is so different for these - they will be the way-bearers if allowed to do so, guided and not suppressed by their peers. You see the younger taking a stance, not fearful of dominant structures. This is good - this is change. Love and Light – Abe.

38.   There have been major migrations of people across the planet in recent years. This cultural mix of diversity has many advantages, and yet it instills fear in many people also. Does not diversity and inter-mixing help to strengthen the collective human vibration in a positive way?

Yes, it does. For you are all but the same, but society can install this division and in this deepen the route of separation. For if this was not so, their structures would fall instantly. They would have no grounds, for they are all built upon the shaky foundations of identity of separation. For if you are all just in conversation to one thing - to yourself - then are you not only trying to point out that 'I am right, and I am also wrong?' It is pure madness - it is a disease of mind, of your vibrational signature. Love and Light – Abe.

39.   We need to bring the sense of the sacred back into our lives. The sense of enchantment and cosmic communion. How can we realise this amongst humanity?

First, recognise your humanity. For when you realise what you truly are, you are humbled. For in the opening up to that of which you are, you realise one thing - that all is the same. There is deep unification in this being - feel right back to this, right back to the core; back to the essence: the life that flows through your veins, the love that opens your heart, the ever-growing knowledge of existence that pulsates and opens up the vibrational signature to so much more. In seeing this unification, you will not be able to restrict your being again. To see that in which it once was, growth is inevitable - and in this humanity is taking a big conscious step forward into a new world. A new way, fearless and open to life. Love and Light – Abe.

40.   It is said that modern life is making us more isolated and more tribal despite our increased connections. How can we change this situation?

We see that you are not to go back in time to a set of isolated communities but a whole network. This is much like the worldwide web but in physicality - a united network of communication all over the planet and this will then expand. One could liken it to, say, your individual brains creating another unified brain being that of the planet - then of being of the cosmos. The neural pathways are created by vibrational resonance, and so within is also that without. Is this of understanding now?

41.   Talking of alternative communities - will it not be vital to find alternative means of localized energy? Do you envision communities moving away from global-grid energy supplies? Isn't this a necessity?

Yes, this is what the work of the community is to be - to become self-sufficient. Clearly, not everyone at the start will envision this. But once they come back to unity, when they are less splintered - hear that we say - for it will be an ongoing evolution like everything else. But being amongst and working together in these communities will only strengthen that in which you truly know - that all is but one. When you see that this way of living can only allow you to thrive, then more and more will join in this new way of being. There are such better ways to harvest your energy on this planet and these communities will do so. They will lead the way in new ways, not only working more in harmony but bringing you back to life - to be able to feel and embrace it again. Finally, you will breathe again. Love and Light – Abe.

42.   Alternative communities have existed in the past, and some still do today. Yet many have been corrupted by greed, egos, power, etc. Can you say more about how you would envision correct relations to exist within and between balanced communities.

It always will have to come back to this for you to go forward - it is like being lost on a path trying to find the way out, then someone will come along and forget also within the distraction of actually being lost. What you have to do is come back to this, knowing first and foremost, otherwise you are but running around in a panic as to what to do and where to go. Stop, realign and readjust. Now, how we envision you to but go about your relations with another; well, that would never be of us to say. For you need to do so this first and then see how it feels; for in this knowing it will be of natural essence to connect. You see, you have but hid yourselves away and gone within - it is but time now to shine, quietly whispering to the ones whom are lost 'I think I know a way out.' With Love and Light – Abe.

43.   There are some communities who prefer the 'simple life' – living sustainably, sometimes with minimal or no technology, living close to the earth. Many of these are good, honest people who prefer to live away from the noise and distractions. Do you feel these communities will grow in popularity? Are these good examples of how to live in today's cluttered and distracting world?

We just said previously that you are but hidden from the world and we see that it has been of benefit. And like we say about the guru on the top of the hill, we would like it to be seen that you share and communicate and interact and but be in life with the new skills and the new ways and ideas. To share this in which you have learnt whilst taking the necessary time to disconnect - not a shouting off the rooftops or preaching but of a whisper to the ones who want but something else, something real. Is this of understanding? See this, implement the what you call the worldwide web in reality, make these vibrational contacts, these new pathways. With much Love and Light – Abe.

We so but want to say also it is not a bad thing to go off and disconnect so long as you at some point come back online. You see this?

4th SERIES

–

SCIENCE & TECHNOLOGY

Hello Abe and thank you for the continued connection. We appreciate this communication. Now we would like to ask you questions concerning the themes of science and technology.

1.   Our science says that our known material universe began with an event they call 'The Big Bang.' How accurate is that? How was the universe created?

Good morning. We are also delighted to have this continued communication. Ah, the big bang - a starting point at which all came into creation. Let me ask you, do you see existence in such a way that there had to be a point of attraction at where it all began? For if all is of one thing then where can you possibly pinpoint a certain point at which it all began? We understand that science has come to this conclusion as they want to see a prominent starting point, but they are also forgetting that what would actually cause this big bang. See it as this, there is vibration, call it a sound, and there are instruments now to receive this vibration and interpret it in any way as such as the mechanism is built. You see, to have a big bang there had to be some sort of starting point at which all came into creation, and although this is true in a sense for your physical world it is not true in a vibrational sense and that in what you truly are. See, if you want to get down to the nitty gritty and see the tiny details then you will honestly see that there is space and nothing, and within this nothing there is everything. And you see that you come from nothing, you play in a world of everything, and then you return to nothing. We are by no means saying that the big bang did not happen and created worlds. But you see, it is not the beginning and there will never be a neat little packaged end for this timeline - that you do so hold onto in your physical existence is not so but a circle, a constant becoming. Love and Light – Abe.

Yes, we can. It is one of connection, of interaction and, like you say, harmonious interrelationships of this one vibration, being transformed into worlds and living beings and stars and planets. You are able to feel love from outside of yourself but all this time just this one thing, this one vibration, spread out experiencing all things across all created timelines and structures and languages. For in this oneness there is everything - and although it looks like nothing in a physical sense, it contains it all. You see, at the beginning - and we use this term very, very loosely but so that you can see that in which we want to get across - if in your sciences now you can grasp that beyond even energy it is vibration. That this is source, that this vibration was the beginning of it all. You see, there was never a big bang in a sense for there were no ears to hear that it was; but of itself, like something that turned itself inside out to allow these things to spill from it. For you see, vibration is of nothing - can you grasp it? You can certainly feel it for you have this physical body to sense in such a way, but you cannot hold it and you will never contain it. The more it spreads, the more it creates and interacts and connects and changes. But see this, it is all but one thing - one truth, one vibration, and you are it. Love and Light — Abe.

3.   When we say that other universes exist within other dimensions, are we saying that they exist within a different vibrational state? How do multiverses form, and how do they relate?

It is so this way. Multidimensional is just a term for multi-vibrations in which you are incapable of experiencing, for in your physical existence you have this point. But see this, you are in a sea of vibratory communication; your body would be over stimulated and burn out quickly if it could sense this all at the same time. This is why evolution is key. It is a slowing down of what you already are - like a fine wine to be sipped and enjoyed and revelled in - to be fully immersed in the experience. Does this answer your question?

4.   If we could shift our vibrational resonance would we be able to gain access to other multi-vibrational realities?

Yes. But see this, it will not flood in. More so, a revealing of the pathway - so long as you can keep taking vibrational steps forward, in trust of that which will come before you. Is this of understanding now?

5.   Our science now agrees on the theory of quantum energy. The quantum plenum, or zero-state, is said to be the formless energy field from which the universe manifests. Isn't this quantum zero-state also Abe?

It is so this way. But hear this - it is also you.

6.   If we are also a part of this zero-state then we have access to incredible energy. How may we manifest this energy - and is this part of our in-form function?

You are able to harness this energy as you evolve, and you evolve by allowing this energy also. It is a transactional interaction, for the energy always has to be equal to the mechanism. It is just this so, for if you draw in too much you will blow the fuse, so to speak. Love and Light – Abe.

7.   Quantum science appears to be the science of
        the future and understanding of quantum field
        effects may revolutionize evolution on this planet.
        What can you say about this?

The quantum field too is best understood as the zero-state, or nothing, for you can get into the idea that all is born from this one something. It is not so - it is a resting point at which all is ready to go again and again. Not for reason, for this wave does not have purpose - it expands and interacts and changes form and no form. It is born and it does but is never not there - for even when the heart stops beating there is a flatline, a resting point is there not? It is a waving, a peak and trough, a high and a low, around and about, and all this time a dance of polarities is really just the dance of one. Do you see this?

8.   Is then the quantum field different from the 'Abe'
        zero-state? Our science says that all energy is
        contained in this quantum state. Yet it is also at
        rest. Could you clarify more on what we call the
        'quantum'?

No, it is not. For if all is one, how can it be so. It is where you say it is resting point - it is where form is called one. You could liken it to the state of drawing things out of a blind bag, like you are pulling something out of thin air, but this is not true for there is never space - and as you evolve you will see this more and more. For you never just pull something from thin air but from an all-inclusive pool of consciousness. Call it quantum, call it Abe, call it you - for all of these answers will be correct. Love and Light – Abe.

9.   The known universe is said to be held together by dark energy, and yet our sciences known very little about this. Could you explain dark energy and its significance?

It is a term we like to call a place at which things cannot be measured, for this is the zero-state. And although we say about the quantum field, this is but too the same thing. It is not different - it has a term, for science have been able to call it something for it is the point or cusp of creation. Now see this, a tube that can stretch out, circle around back upon itself, all but the same one tube but points of just the same thing - the tube. Is this of understanding?

10.   Are you saying that dark energy, zero-state, and Abe are all the same thing – the same state?

Yes. For what is in darkness is just but that which has not seen the light - that being of perception, of the interaction, the splitting apart. Is this of understanding?

11.	What are the functions of black holes?

Black holes are just points of different vibratory connections. See this, like the workings of the brain it is necessary for your brain to evolve to make certain neural pathways, connections. This is but so the same for black holes. Is this understood?

12.	Could you explain a little more about how black holes function in the cosmos?

Black holes are but the connectors, the points at which when vibrationally aligned will open to reveal a connection, a joining up. See, these pathways are being created within so will then be created without too, to reveal more when the vibrational alignment is connected. When points are joined up, like within the brain, you create a different perception - do you not? Well, this is so for black holes - same thing but outside of yourselves. See, in the resonation you open up more, creating more pathways, until it all just comes back to one. Is this of understanding?

13.	The galactic core is said to be an 'engine of energy' – how does this energy affect cosmic evolution?

The galactic core is but the inside of the outside. It is but the centre, but also the very outer. It is not really an effect on cosmic evolution but a part of it. You see, in this world of polarity you have to see a grinder and engine room - but is not so. It could very well be a large attraction point like, but you see all is attraction, inter-relational. It is things even beyond this that are keeping it in point of attraction. Your science looks on expansion and should rather be looking at vibration, which is in essence nothing. But understand this, you are then of understanding of all and the interrelationship of things. We would like to say one thing: that these too are gateways - not for other places but for larger and larger connections vibrationally to be made; a piecing together if you will. Love and Light – Abe.

14.   Much has been said about the 'galactic alignment' – is this an important phenomenon and how would it affect processes on this planet?

Yes. You see, the pathways are being carved out - they are of a vibrational essence. All the points are there to make these connections. We say but one thing and it is this - a web of consciousness infinitely expanding. Is this of understanding?

15.   Do certain galactic/cosmic alignments have an effect on human consciousness? Do such alignments form a part of the process of planetary evolution?

It is so, for it creates a shift; and in that shift you then create a shift and then back and forth and around and around. You see, it is all communicating vibrationally, and always has. You see, there is a conversation that has been going on - all you have to do is allow and listen. Love and Light – Abe.

16.   The scientist-inventor Nikola Tesla knew about the energies of vibration. Was he accessing the unified field? Could you comment upon the work of Nikola Tesla?

He was but a person that was open, that could understand particularly vibration - although has been recently more understood - and was taking this infinite power that everyone is capable of. You see, the people who seem to be ahead of their times are usually seen as crazy for they have allowed this energy to flow forth and in this made the necessary connections. They have evolved. You see, in allowing this you enable it, and when you enable it you allow it to manifest in physical form. You are making a necessary connection, and in this evolving. But you must see that this connection is but never lost; it's just that you are on but a different frequency. You are blocking it out - you are of material frequency and life wants to cause you to allowcosmic frequency. Is this of a sufficient answer to this?

17.   You said that 'life wants to cause you to allow cosmic frequency' – is this then how we develop and evolve, by allowing cosmic frequency to manifest through us and upon the planet?

It is so. But hear this, you are but never apart from it. You are but blocking it out and shutting it down, for you do not understand that part of yourselves. And some who do, have over-conceptualised and tied down something that so just wants to flow. You see, you can still be you – 'you' just have to rhythm up, get in tune, by stopping and listening. Love and Light – Abe.

18.	To clarify on the functioning of black holes - you said that they operate like inside of a brain, as if creating new neural pathways. Would black holes be like cosmic synapses, creating pathways to stars and aligning with them vibrationally and energetically?

This is exactly so: like one giant brain, one giant consciousness - all but one thing making its way back to this. Love and Light – Abe.

19.	There are many irregularities concerning Earth's moon. Some theories speculate that our planet's moon is an artificial structure. Also, that there are other artificial moons/structures in our solar system. Could you comment on this?

Good morning. Ah, the moon as an artificial structure. If we are completely honest, and we want this communication to always be so, then we would say it is nonsense. There will always be theories, for words are just thoughts, and everyone is entitled to their own view. But see here, the world was flat until you found the necessary items to connect up and communicate and interact better with your world - and in this discovering yourselves. For it is always inter-relational and you can only discover and connect the points when the two points are at resonation to one another. And vibration is the key to creating these cosmic neural pathways - as within, so without. Love and Light – Abe.

20.	Although humans reportedly landed on the moon in 1969, there has been no further manned exploration of the solar system. Could you comment on this?

As we said above, the points of connection have to resonate. But see, that they are really not apart at all - it is only apart because of the dissonance between them. It is not because you are separated at all; it is that there is a clouding - a mist, a fog, an engaged line or fault on the line would be a better term - that does not enable you to connect and receive. We keep going back to this. But the brain, as you get older and experience more through life, new pathways are created. This is the same with cosmic pathways - the more you allow, the more you see. It is always equal in resonance, and discovering your vibratory essence is key to this shift in consciousness, which in turn will create more pathways. It is so tightly interwoven. Is this of understanding? We would like to add that there has not been more exploration for you are shifting as a species and maybe, just maybe, it is time to discover yourselves fully before you could, and would, be able to create new pathways. Love and Light – Abe.

21.   There has been talk recently of attempting to colonize Mars. Is this a positive – or necessary - move forward for our species evolution? Is our species ready to move off Earth?

We do not feel that it is time to do this yet. As we say, we would see it be for this to benefit the cosmos at all you would really as a whole species have connected more - united within and without. For you see, if you are to do this at present then are you not just bringing more dissonance? We do not feel it is the right time, for you need to discover all that you are and piece it back together. For if, as a species, you are wanting this colonization from a splintered mind then this will not enable you to move forward. This step, we feel, should always come from a place of unification for it to be of any use or benefit to your species. Love and Light – Abe. We would like to add that just like the brain, the pathways, the connections have to be clear. In this, meaning vibratory flow within is of utmost importance. Is this of understanding?

22.   Yes, it makes sense that a species should not
        consider further colonization in the cosmos until it is
        unified within. Is this the same understanding with
        other intelligent species in the cosmos? There is
        speculation here that other cosmic species may
        wish to do us harm - that is, they are in dissonance
        and not in harmony or unity. Could you comment?

It is not the other species at all, not the ones that are further
along evolved, for they could of only evolve by seeing this
unification. For in the seeing of this is the way you move
forward - you evolve. We would be more inclined to say that
a species that is splintered would do far more harm. Love and
Light – Abe.

23.   In terms of species evolution, there can only be a
        continued development when there is a
        recognition of unification and a unified mind. Any
        species which would wish to cause dissonance
        would be less evolved. Is this correct?

Yes, this is so. But you see, if your very planet is but evolving
too then you will have to shift, or you will not be of resonance.
This, meaning, you have to take the jump at some point from
a crumbling tower. With Love and Light – Abe.

24.   You talk about new 'cosmic pathways'
       opening up as we make the resonating
       connections. Is this a way of saying that the
       cosmos - or further 'unknowns' - will make
       themselves available to us when we show, as a
       species, that we are ready? If you like, we could
       say that we create our own quarantine until we
       can prove we are ready to move out?

You will always create tighter and tighter restrictions when you are of dissonance, of resistance - it is always so. You create your own little boxes through fear of loss of control, but this needs to be loosened now. You, as a species, have to see this unification, firstly piecing yourself back together - taking back what society has told you and the way in which you have been conditioned. In turn, this will allow you to allow new connections. Your circles will get larger and expansion will come naturally. But it will only ever be from this place of unification. Why make your life harder by forcing pathways when by allowing would be not only easier but more harmonious? Love and Light – Abe.

25.   You stated before that the human body will
       merge with technology that will result in longer
       life spans. This issue of the human-cyborg is very
       controversial. Is this biology-technology merger a
       natural flow in the evolutionary process? Can
       you talk more on this?

It will be a natural flow and would be beneficial if it is coming from these unforced pathways of evolutionary connection. We are not asking you to sit around and wait. But firstly, know all that you are for if you can really grasp this as a whole species it will surely be a quantum leap for you in evolutionary terms. Love and Light – Abe.

26.	Human scientists are experimenting more with biotechnology, such as DNA modification and gene sequencing. There is the probability here of modifying the human body. This is controversial for many people. Is this an inevitable part of our species evolution?

We would like to say too that if, and always, it is coming from a place of unification. For the splintered human is just that – splintered. For if you only had part of the ingredients to make a cake it would not work, it would not be complete - and in this would it even be a cake? You see, there is great intention of making the cake but if you do not have the complete ingredients to make it then you may well end up with something that was not intentional at all. Is this of understanding? The grounding - the unified human - is one to carve greatness into the world; especially into a world that is so splintered. But there is great hope, for all across the planet unification is appearing even in the darkest corners. Love and Light – Abe.

27.	Technology is advancing at a rapid pace. We are at a crossroads of where biological life is merging with technology. Some people are calling this a new 'post-human' era. Is it a normal evolutionary drive to replace carbon-based life-forms with technology-machine intelligence? What can you say about this?

It is not, no. More so, we would like to say as to support the biological functioning if need be. But we see that the way in which you are going is not from a place of unification - of knowing of this vibrational essence to everything. You really cannot delay this any longer for your species is on the cusp of moving forward. This is why we have continued to manifest, to say 'hold on – let's get this part right first and then when we truly understand this, then we can move forward.' We are not saying that you should listen to us at all, but listen and feel to yourselves. Understand yourselves first and foremost before you take a step forward - from a place of love and understanding and not from a place as to which to be a winner of the race. Love and Light – Abe

28.	We agree that our species evolution should not be a race or competition. Yet it seems as if there is another race between the evolution of our awareness about our unitary essence and technological development. If our awareness does not advance sufficiently, doesn't this indicate for problematic futures?

They can only do so if you are not wise, if you are asleep to it. If you don't play the game, then there is no game to play - is it not true? You see, it will cause dissonance for if there is dissonance within then surely it be shown in your very existence and in all you do. Harmonize within and see that this will shine out. You see, when you have a light it cancels out the darkness. It does not eradicate it, but light is shone upon what was only once unseen. We are not saying you should be a perfect species, for there is no such ideal - but to know truly and understand truly, without a doubt, that in which you are. It is not so to say all should listen and lord this information over each and every one of you. No, but to awaken that little spark to nudge the heart as if to say 'life is here, it is waiting.' That is all we can ever wish to do. The rest is really up to yourselves. Love and Light – Abe. We would also like to say that this should never be preached or say that we are right, that this is truth. But to allow you to feel these words in the center of your very being for you to know that what we speak of as truth.

29.   Have there been other planets that passed through an advanced technological evolution? If so, how did they experience this process?

There is, and there have – yes. Every planet is differing in its needs of these differing technological advancements. But see this, it is all to be used and only to enhance the organism. So be very wary if your species is using these in ways to control and manipulate, for they are not the purpose for someone who is coming from a place of unification at all. We have seen this battle before, but it can be overcome by knowing that in which you are - knowing your power and place of resonance. Controlling and manipulation will always try to push forth. In some sense, it is in the knowing of what you are is where your power really lies. Love and Light – Abe.

30.	There are international efforts to develop forms of artificial intelligence. This could be incredibly positive for the evolution of human civilization or highly problematic. What can you say about artificial intelligence?

Again, we feel like a stuck record; but this is only truth. It needs to be from this place of unification always. We see that there are people in power and who have the money and resources to do this now who one could say is not of unification and are very much in it for the race. But you see, you always think that you are powered by such people when in reality it is the other way around. The masses are awakening to this dissonance - they are claiming back their power. Artificial intelligence will be of benefit if, like we say, it is a tool, an enhancement to the lives of others. Otherwise, it is of no use for it will be in the wrong hands. Love and Light – Abe.

We are by no means saying that this transition to unification will be a complete easy ride, for there will be destruction and dismantling of old structures. But see this, it is making way for these new connections that have unified within and therefore

can only unify without, claiming back your evolutionary stance.
Love and Light – Abe.

31. With increased automation of our lives more and
     more people will be compelled to find answers for
     the role and function of the human being. How
     can people seek for meaning in an increasingly
     controlled world?

Meaning is always that in which you make it, always. It is never
outside of you. You have been conditioned in such a way that
this is always sought outside of yourselves, but it is not so. One
can find meaning in the seemingly mundane where others it is
doing great. What we would like to say that all meaning is, is
really just connection. Like the universe wants to know itself
through itself, so this is true for you. Connect, be open, be true.
Love and Light – Abe.

32. Powerful technologies – such as cyber and bio-
     technologies – are increasingly in the hands of
     small groups or even individuals. Will this create a
     dissonance of power relations that could create
     greater uncertainty amongst humanity?

If people are wise to what they are, if they stand strong in the
knowing of this unification, then they would not even entertain
the game at all. It is only when you are splintered that you are
powerless. There will be a struggle of power between people
claiming theirs back and the few who remain to want to
manipulate and control. And they will do so through fear, but

the harmonization of such will balance out. We are never claiming of what your species see as all good - this is a world of polarity. But bringing back to balance is key - centering yourselves first. Love and Light – Abe.

33.   Virtual/Augmented reality and video games are increasingly popular amongst the young people. These interactions also have the capacity to re-wire our brains, do they not? Some people are worried about young people's fixation with such activities. Could you comment on this?

Yes, it does but re-wire and re-adjust. It is about balance. But see this, they are of understanding that this is so a game - for the ones that are of entrapment are really the ones stuck in a reality and are unaware that they are but playing a game at all. Is this of understanding?

34.   What advice could you give us about the development and use of technologies?

The only advice we would like to give is use them to enhance life and be very wary if a technological advancement creates dissonance rather than connection, for this will only be moving you away further from the truth, enabling the few to keep this power and redeeming you as powerless. All technological advancement, if more and more become unified, will enable you to explore yourselves, your world, and the cosmos more.

And in this waking up, more and more people creating greater and greater neural pathways within and without in the cosmos. This will, of course, need your species to evolve, to advance in some way. But always it should be of promoting connection and pathways. With much Love and Light – Abe.

We would also like to add, if you are prompting us to state what technological advancements will occur, then we would like to say that we are understanding that technology is advancing at a rapid pace and it seems to be very much still in the hands of the few who may use such technologies to create dissonance. More so, what we have to say is that it will only be balanced out again or taken back if people are wise to it - not everyone, for like a wave it will spread anyway. But for these new pathways to be formed there has to be that first step - that first one or few who will walk it first and say, 'look, it is not so scary as you think.' Do you understand why we talk so much about getting this key foundation set first? We leave you now with much love and light and great gratitude to be able to come forth. Love and Light – Abe.

35.   Life extension is now a major research area. Some
         scientists wish to eradicate death. This sounds
         good, but is it wise to try to eliminate the natural
         dying of our bodies? This could be problematic for
         vibrational signatures as well as over-population.
         Could you comment on this?

It will always be of your sciences and technological
establishments that want to eradicate the natural processes of
life. And although it is seen as a good thing to prolong life, we
do so feel it should be more of a natural process. But hear this,
we are not at all discounting your advancement as a species, and
although life expectancy will be prolonged due to technological
advancements and the morphing of biological and technical,
we do so feel that in a biological sense it should still be of a
natural process. It is also so that you are changing in form with
these new vibrations, so there will also be a natural evolutionary
process to your being. But as we see it, you cannot rush this
process too far forward. Of course, you can push the
boundaries of life, but what we want to say is that it must always
take in this whole picture. Now, we understand that you would
very much like to prolong your experience in physical form.
But we also see the need not to meddle in it too much, for you
will upset the natural rhythm if pushed too far and that could
be catastrophic - for not only you but to that of the whole
cosmos. You see that there is a fine line between enhancing and
completely dominating, controlling, and forcing life, for all life
is a balancing act and really you must see this place of
unification as we see it. To advance much more balanced,

much more smarter, and much more in flow, trying not to cause further dissonance. Love and Light – Abe.

36.   Following on from the above, there was a news report released today stating that birth rates had radically fallen in the last half a century. Perhaps natural processes will adjust for such things as population and we don't need to try to overtly socially manage this?

It is true that you do need to take a step back at some point to allow balance to appear. Now see this, balance can look destructive and chaotic like things are far from balance, for your social constructs have built their buildings upon changeable foundations. You see that you as humans in your own lives - for example, you do not know when things will change and take a different course. You see life has this funny way of changing direction within a heartbeat - come back to yourself, feel back into your bodies. Bring all those vibrational attachments back in and just see, even if for just a moment, in this deep rest. Even if just momentarily, you will have a deep sense of the world and your part within it. You will see that there is a time for doing and there is a time to sit and just watch the grass grow. Love and Light – Abe.

37.   Time, as we measure it, is a linear path, based on
         solar movement and planetary effects.
         Understandably, time as we experience it is a local
         phenomenon. Yet there is also much speculation
         on the science of time- travel. Could you say
         something about how 'time' is experienced or
         recognized throughout the cosmos?

It is very much of linear process, yes, in your physical existence. For in a sense, it is in harmony for you at this stage in time in your evolutionary process. You see time as around and around on your clocks, but as a line of points at to which can be recorded too. Now, which one could it be? That time is of a circular pattern re- repeating itself, or could it be a long line in which things appear upon and are recorded and dated? But you come to know that time is only but a social construct; to say 'I was here, and I can prove it' because, you see, I existed from one time to another. It was really a mere measurement of existence of individual things at differing times. Now, what we say is - if you took away your clocks and your timelines for a mere moment you would see that it is only here, now. And although we do not like the concept of 'now,' for it has been over-used, it is but a statement of continuous becoming, and you are never apart from it. The functioning of your vibrational signature allows you to ponder upon the future by thinking about the past. But you see, you are here with it - there is nowhere to get to. So long as you can see that and not be attached to future or longing for past - that you are merely here with life and able to do these wondrous things within this time-space reality. You see, we are never here to say 'be here' for it is a wondrous gift to be able to think of the future and mull over past experience - that is being human and being of physical form. It is the attachment to race ahead or drag yourselves back to what once was. You see that there is no time, just a becoming, and to state that there is a now and you should be in it is also a false premise, a past - for the moment you try to become present it has already passed, has it not? Throughout the whole of the cosmos you experience time differently. Some, no time at all - just an interaction of being. And some that have made these new pathways through evolutionary process and vibrational connection to allow them to jump time - time in regards to your measurement - of the one thing, the one happening, the one constant and infinite becoming. Love and Light — Abe.

38.　　　As we shift into a new phase of human civilization we will require new forms of energy extraction and distribution. Scientists are working hard on nuclear fusion/fission, hydrogen power, and similar forms that use atomic elements. Yet is there a way to utilize the quantum or zero energy to provide for our needs? Isn't it time that we understood how to access new energy forms that are cosmic rather than planetary?

It is, and you will step into this process only when you are of full understanding of vibration and unification. There is infinite power in this source of zero-state. But you see, you can harness this for yourselves for this too is of you and from the world around. No longer will you have to rely upon physical, material sources to power your world, but to look to vibrational attraction, for this is the key that holds much power. But hear this, you must also firstly - and this is of great importance - come to this place of unification for this power could be used for destruction rather than benefiting yourselves as a species. Is this of understanding now?

39.   Are we likely to discover and utilize a science of vibrations within this century? Where will science go from here? What can we expect next?

Science is moving forward, and they are becoming more and more so aware of the unseen and even the unmeasurable. But hear this, they have not yet fully unified this, for they are still very much separate things. When science can see the vibrational element is really no differing from that of your physical existence it will go much further. It will make these pathways, these neural pathways, clear to join up. If they could firstly join up matter and vibration, well, science will excel and in this will cause you to join up the dots within. We cannot say a specific time for it is all about the allowance of this connection, which is trying to pave a new path. We see that it will be of great significance over the next 10 years or so in the discovery of moving forward to a more unified existence, and in this an emergence of, one could say, spirit and matter. But hear this, when science knows undoubtedly that these two things were never of separation at all - that there was merely a fault on the line, a contamination of sorts – well, it will be of fast movement forwards - of infinite expansion of mind, a more cosmic communicative system. For you see, in the move forward your brain expands; it creates new pathways and in this you create this within the cosmos too. And with this you become more of a communicative race without the need of material substance. Is this of understanding?

40.   Some popular scientists are publishing books about how to create colonies on other planets and interstellar travel, etc. They say this is the future of humanity. Are they preparing the human species in advance? Or is this a misconceived belief and a result of the splintered mind?

We would like to say it is of advancement, but we see so much that there is very much still this splintered mind. See this, an allowance of vibration to a splintered mind, the flow, is there - it can never not be. But it is but falling upon an object that will split apart and not fully understand this unification. Now, if you were to allow, and also understand, unification it will flow through the process. You would be the channel that brings connections rather than the one that allows, and then sifts, and sorts, and places through your own vibrational signature. And although we always say that it is not to be rid of it, is in the knowing of when to put it aside and to be of service to yourself, and in this to the whole. Is this of understanding?

41.	Our science still believes that space travel will be accomplished by forms of energy propulsion. Is it not more probable that humanity will explore the cosmos through extended consciousness rather than physical bodies?

We do so see this, yes, for now. But it will be of sorts to come that you will not need apparatus to visit, for your bodies will be differing. See it like this, you hear of near-death experiences to be that some see God or enter heaven and see loved ones. This is but the vibrational signature not leaving the body. For we do not see start and end, or that of a soul. This is why we use vibrational signature for it is what one would call mind too. They have these experiences, for even though the body is dead the consciousness is not. So, the vibrational signature is back into the zero-state although never being apart - it just does not have the channel in which to express through. It is into this cosmic consciousness, if you will, just a different state. The reason that people can remember this and, although being clinically dead in your material existence, there is a point in which vibrational alignment or resonance is still to that of this body and its conditionings. We understand that this may of gone off of the question quite a bit, but what we are really trying to express is that the more pathways that are created through you, and then within the cosmos, the less need there will be to explore in a physical sense for you will see that consciousness is but free to travel and is not as constrained as you once thought so. Love and Light – Abe.

42.   The advancement of computation has given us
        the perspective that the cosmos operates similar
        to a kind of program. Some people speculate that
        we are living inside of a grand cosmic computer
        program and that our lives are like a simulation.
        Would this be a suitable analogy?

We would rather but see it more so as an evolutionary process, more so a brain. You see, we talk about these neural pathways and we mean that for both on the material level and also that of the cosmos level. Is this of understanding? For you see, if there is just one thing and you are it, then what is within is also without on a larger scale - a going back if you will to the Russian doll analogy. Love and Light — Abe.

43.   Many people now experience synchronicities in
        their lives, and 'signs' as if - they say - the
        'universe' is speaking to them. Are there such
        interventions where messages are placed into the
        material realm?

Not so much a placement but of an allowance. But you see, you have to be aware of them too. But hear this, some people get so caught up in the signs and synchronicities they grab a hold of them; as in a way to know and therefore control or resist certain experience. You see, there is always a knowing of sorts if you are allowing; and allowing is knowing. And then in this the universe is then always in communication with you. Love and Light — Abe.

44.   New technologies are likely to be more accessible
        to the elites - especially such things as genetic
        enhancement. Isn't there a possibility that the
        human race will be divided by this rather than
        unified?

It is so a possibility. But you see, are you not then putting continued power to those at the top, so to speak? You see, they are interested in power and at present power is money. This will shift course, and of course there will be someone who will want to manipulate whatever commodity is of utmost importance for your survival as a species. You will see that in the shifting of yourselves there will be a shifting of power. It will be placed back into the hands of the many rather than the few. But hear this, it will be a struggle for you have allowed it for such a long time and have left many things dormant and gathering dust. It is not a battle of power as such - more so, a shift. Is this of understanding? We would also like to add that a unified being is of utmost importance now for this is where you will gain all your power back - all your pieces that have been splintered for so long. Yes, there will be technological advancements and no doubt be people that will want to control and manipulate. With this we are not stating a euphoric existence but a real one. But you see, the more and more people that are understanding and knowing of this unification - this vibration in which you are being shifted to resonate with, to understand - the more these structures will not be able to withhold. For you see, the animals that became extinct were the ones that could not resonate to their systems; and therefore, could not continue into the new vibrational evolution. Is this of understanding now?

45.   To bring back power to the masses, we need to shift our vibrationary state – to drop our social conditionings, our ego, our fixed identities, and to allow a connection for consciousness to flow. If people can resonate to a new state of being, then so will our social systems shift and evolve. Is this what you are saying?

Yes, this is true. But see, these things do not have to be dropped permanently and cannot. One could liken it to a good clear-out of such, then put back once you have given the shelving a good dusting. Is this of understanding?

46.   It seems obvious that technology is now a permanent part of our human lives. At the same time there will be a need to be closer to Nature - maybe a wish to return   to more agrarian lifestyles. How can this seeming contradiction between high technology and pastoral living be balanced?

It can be used to harness this zero-state - this vibrational attraction - for it can power your life in such a way that there will be no need to rip apart your world to create more power. It will also be in such a way that your own being is the power point and there will be no need for others to control and manipulate. For how could one manipulate if all you need is all you have right now? In this it will create more of a unified field of communication, not only in your physical existence but that of the cosmos too. Love and Light – Abe.

47.   Scientists have constructed a complex particle accelerator – the Hadron collider – to search for new particles and to examine unsolved questions in physics. Some people view these experiments as risky. Is this a wise way to operate in order to know the cosmos better?

You see, there will always be things that come up for you to scrutinize and pinpoint a point of your existence. It is done so in a way to utilize power; to create points at which this power can be utilized. Which way that seems to go is unclear. For as we like to say, a splintered mind/being is far more likely to use this for their own gains rather than using it for a more unified purpose. We see that scientists are getting the focus to smaller and smaller particles to enable them to figure out your material existence. But see this, the more and more focused it becomes the more it is pinpointed, the more splintered your existence becomes. Open up and you will see the greatest power source, and in this you will discover yourselves. We are not saying that you should not become focused on the details, but firstly you need to open up, then to re-adjust. Love and Light – Abe.

48.   Scientists note that our local galaxy – which we
        call the Milky Way – contains around a billion
        planets that are 'Earthlike' in their properties. Our
        strongest telescope can spot about 100 million
        galaxies in the visible universe. In an earlier
        communication you stated that there are only 5
        planets in the cosmos, including ours, that is at an
        advanced stage of evolution. Isn't this a small
        number compared to the potentials?

It is. But see this, there are more that harbour life in a different way. What we are saying is that there is only a small amount that are in relation to your type of physicality of being. This is not to mean that you are a minority. Far from that, but a small part of differing life spread across all of the cosmos. You see, it is only now as technology has evolved that you are discovering what has been in your deepest oceans for millennia. Is this of understanding?

49.   Contact with other advanced intelligences, say
        our scientists, is more likely to come from powerful
        electronic brains rather than humanoid,
        biological species. How close is this to the truth?

We would like to say that it is not so, for you always have that in which you need. See this, you are always receiving; you are never apart from this. It is only in your vibrational signature that is contaminating connection in a way. But you see, it would not serve you either to be rid of it. It is always about the whole, the unification of things. If you can really get to grips with this then there will be no limits. But you see, you have been contaminated with the notion that you are a physical being and even though this is so there is much more to you than that. It is in the resonance of allowing your being to accept and allow new forms, new pathways, new ways of communication. If you do not understand this unification, then it will not serve you to open up, for it will cause dissonance of vibrations in which you hold. Is this of understanding?

50.   How can we build up, or develop, our means on communication with the cosmos and other non-terrestrial intelligences?

Trust in what you are, knowing of this unified system - allowing vibrational resonance, allowing open heart communication. But see this, before you are to try this be sure for it to be firmly rooted into your being, into all that you do on this level first. Love and Light – Abe.

51.   Science sees physical evolution on the earth as related to environmental factors, including phases of glaciation. But are not phases of consciousness 'directed' and managed as evolutionary impulses upon the earth?

You see, the Earth evolves in physicality and then the species upon that planet have no choice but to move with it. You see, your planet is evolving, and you are doing so in unison. See it like this, you are at a place of work and they put in a new technological advancement to help be more productive. They get rid of the old system and install a new one. Now the workers will have to adapt, will have to learn new ways of being. If not, they could be let go of for they will not be beneficial to the whole operation. Is this of understanding? We are not trying to denounce your part as human beings for it is a true gift. But we are merely trying to put forth that when your planet shifts you have no other choice but to shift with it, and this goes further and further out until zero-state again, and back around and re-creating and changing form and no form. It is so tightly intertwined but always at the core is pure consciousness, just reflecting and retracting and shifting and dancing. Is this of understanding?

52.   Are you saying that past human species went extinct because they were unable to adjust to the earth's evolving shifts and resonance?

Yes, this is what we are but saying. For something to grow - and this is such for you as individuals - some things have to be dropped, they cannot go forward on the same paths. Like the seed that wanted to grow so much, it bust apart all that it was and in this had taken on another form. Is this of understanding?

53.   Technology is often regarded as referring to
        mechanical-type devices. Is there not also a
        'spiritual technology' whereby we can develop
        our internal senses. Perhaps even re-wire our brains
        and nervous system? What would you say about
        this?

For is not technological, or as you state 'mechanical-type devices,' still but an expression of this, of this one thing? For it has come through but the physical organism - through consciousness. What makes the complete difference between them is what vibration it is being filtered through - splintered or unified?

54.   The science of intention and manifestation is both
        recognized and yet similarly ignored by many.
        How is internal intention related to external
        manifestation in our reality?

It is but a filter of consciousness you can allow what is meant to be for you. For you see, it has been a big thing for so long and has been made such a big fuss of, and in this you really have contaminated the line. The pathways have been stopped dead in their tracks. For you have tried to be positive and although it may have its benefits it is very much splintered and much cause of dissonance. We are not saying at all to be passive but unification in oneself is much more a powerful force in the world than a splintered vibration. You can have an intention, you always will for your physical existence. But see this, allow it to come - loosen up the grips of what is meant to be, for your very essence knows the path and you have to trust in that. Once more, open up that heart and allow. With Love and Light – Abe.

55.   We feel that science and technology are focusing too much upon the externals of physical existence, whereby we need now to focus on the intangible, non-physical aspects if we are to successfully develop as a species. Could you comment on this?

It is true, and this is what we mean also in the taking it back to the bare bones. For you are stripping all condition away, which is very much a physical thing, to reach back to this zero-state, and say 'now we're gathering things all back together.' For in this nothing, in this unseen, non-physical part of existence, is the key to many leaps forward as a species - and creating new neural pathways within and without. Is this of understanding now?

56.   Thank you Abe, for your patience with us. We hope to continue this communication and further allow this understanding. Is there anything else you would wish to communicate before we finish this session?

We are glad to be discussing such things and is well and good to ask these questions for they are of importance and are of depth to communicate well that in which we want to put forth. We do hope that this is to continue, and we see things aligning for next steps to be taken. We wish for you to connect and follow your own guidance for that too is but us and also of you. We would like to say but one thing and that is we really want you to see what a true gift it is to be in physical form. And although we try to walk in the middle by neither being overly positive as to delude you of a perfect future, we do not either want to instil fear for this is not our purpose. Our true purpose is to hand it all back - all the constraints that have been put upon you by others and all those that you have put upon yourselves. We hope to continue this communication. With much Love and Light — Abe.

5th SERIES

—

HUMANITY:

where are we now
& where are we going?

1.   Many people consider humanity to be at
         a crossroads where a breakthrough or breakdown
         is more sensitive. To survive this phase will depend
         on our state of consciousness and whether we shift
         quick enough from a splintered to a unified mind?
         What can you say about this?

Yes, this is but true that evolution is one of conscious unity. See it like this, your consciousness is like the glue that will piece what you really are back together again, if you so allowed it. But your vibrational signature but separates and boxes things up. This is due to your social conditioning. You see, it blinkers out this state of being in order to make you a good citizen. Seldom do people allow this into their everyday conscious experience, and in this they have the blinkers on. They do not have the full picture. They do not operate at full capacity, and to live a life in such a way - a life that could be so much more - is the greatest shame of your human experience. But see this, you can only have a breakthrough if you have a breakdown of old paradigms; and if old is crumbling then it paves way for new pathways, new connections. And in this breakdown, there will be great breakthrough as people will be searching within themselves for something that resonates - something that sticks, something that makes them so feel human again. With Love and Light — Abe.

You see, it does not work in such a way for it is in unison - not one to full vibrational capacity, then other; no, but an inter-relational nudging. You see, there is a lot to be said already for vibrational resonance, for people are changing and you can see there is much balance within. The reason for us to come forth is because we see that this resonance is tipping the scales again in a way that people are still engrossed in their own vibrational signatures. For they are understanding this unified field, but they are shifting to make it into something special, something above and beyond, something that you have to aspire to or make yourselves equal to - you have to be better, to not get angry or sad. But you see, this would not be of balance at all and would not be of a human experience. The only way to unity is accepting the light and the dark, the love and the hate, as but the same thing because within this unity you realise that you are perfectly imperfect, and that is wonderful. Is this of understanding? When you ask but of a timescale to this, we would be so inclined to say within the next century. For you see, to really uproot what has been common knowledge for humanity needs to also be uprooted from the minds of humanity, and this will take time for people will feel a gaping hole where what once stood a statue of self, and you had built your whole world around it. But you see, this gap does not need to be filled again but to allow life to flow uninstructed through your being. We would like to strip things back to the name of 'no name' for even after all this communication with us you too will even have to drop us to see this truth also. Love and Light – Abe.

3.	We dream about the future. Some people say they can see into the future. Surely the future is a set of potentials rather than a fixed destiny? What can you say about this?

We would be inclined to say that it is but both. Now see this, there are fixed outcomes as an inevitability. For example, you throw an egg at a wall - in its natural state it is going to smash. But there are many differing factors that could be changed in order to give a different outcome if you're consciously aware. Say, for example, you make a target you are more certain as to where that would hit. Or, if you did so boil the egg first it would most probably not smash the egg at all; well, not in the way it would do so as before. Is this of understanding?

4.	Humans are dreamers. What happens to our vibrational signature during the sleep state? Do our dreams have significance?

This is but the time that you give up this vibrational signature. You are at resting point and you see you are back to zero-state - you are unified. We would rather but see dreaming as waking up, for you are so conditioned to be active and doing. We are not saying that this should be such a way for your physical existence, but of unified collaboration, conscious and unconscious - the whole picture. For in this state of being you are allowing and also able to act. You are aware and also allowing - this is resonance of your very being. This is resonance to your planet, and this is resonance to the universe. Love and Light – Abe.

5.	Life seems to be so highly complex and yet based upon some very simple laws. What are these laws?

The laws are ————————for there are no laws. For the moment you speak you have taken it away from that in which it really is. But we see this may not suffice as good for us to give an explanation of how the world or cosmos works. So, we say this - it is all, and will always ever be, a vibrational resonance. This is true across all times, all space; and when resonance happens, physicality is created. You have long forgotten your vibrational essence and how it is tying and binding itself to things and places and people and experiences - and future outcomes and past problems. One simple thing; one thing – vibration. Remember this and you really do remember yourselves. Bring this into your conscious minds and you will see it in all that you interact with. Is this of understanding?

6.	We have been told before by other teachings to 'raise our vibration.' It sounds good. Yet it also sounds abstract and New Age. How can we explain to the average person to raise their vibration?

You allow it. Strip it back; all the conditions in which you have put upon life, upon yourselves, and upon others. Give life room to move again within you, for there isn't a state to get to - it is here. It's just that you have the blinkers on, the social blinkers - take those off and allow all that you are. See the unity in all that you do, and your vibration will be nothing but resonance to your world, to each other. In this you will be creating heart-to-heart connections in all that you do. With Love and Light – Abe.

7.   If a person begins to shift their vibrational resonance, this will affect others in whom they come into contact with – like a transmitter? Isn't this one aspect of how change can manifest, by positively infecting others, so to speak?

You can do so. But see this, if their vibrational essence is one of pure resistance then it will at first not have any flow. But hear this, it is of not forcing at all but of you continuously resonating at that at which you are - and in this it will break through at some point, weathering away at that contamination. The only thing you can do is not allow it to contaminate yours. If so, it is but a good idea to strengthen your own connection before trying to change that of others. Is this of understanding now?

You see, like we said before you have been conditioned in such a way to block it out and to hurry up and just get on with it. For this will make you easy to handle, predictable, and safe - but this is not true. In this conditioning you have become more and more disconnected. For a splintered mind creates just that - a splintered world, and in that a splintered cosmos. To move forward you have to understand that this is how it is. That it is all but a unified field - and we are not bad, we are it. In this realization that we are it, in this deep knowing that 'oh yes, it's all the same and I am it too,' you let up the character. It is not so important you let yourselves and others off the hook. But see this, it is a process, it is a becoming. Of this there are lots of conditioning to unwrap. Is this of understanding?

To shift into a state of knowing then, you have to be allowing. Your current paradigm is one of resistance to what is not physical, and in this you shut out vibration. You shut out yourselves, tightening the conscious experience, restricting it. The only way to allow is to rest. Just for now, gather in all the wires of intention, the hooks of belief - reel them back in just for now and rest. Gather and recalibrate the system – harmonize, unite.

9.   There will be many people who will consider it crazy that a 'unified zero-state field' called Abe is speaking to them. What would you say to them?

Ahh, yes. It would be so such a way because you have been conditioned in such a way as to shut this out, for it is not of service, to keep order and obedience. But you see, the name is not of importance at all. For like we said, even after this connection and writings - and there will be but plenty more writings - we would say drop it too, for you are allowing zero-state to come forth and in this you are allowing all that you are. You are allowing pure consciousness to express in physical form. This is not available to just the few but to each and every one, if they do so allow. Drop it all and allow. Is this of understanding now?

10.   Some may say that the age of religion is over. We no longer need the crutches of   intermediary teachings when we can access Source directly. Is humanity moving into an era of conscious communication with Source? Is this necessary to evolve further as a species on this planet?

It is this way, yes. You are but moving into a different pathway, a conscious evolution. It is so that in the loosening of your own individual vibrational signatures you allow more and more of this energy in - this vibration. We do not want you to be rid of your vibrational signature, for this will never be so. But you see, in the allowance of the new vibration it shakes loose the contamination that has been considered your vibrational signature for so long. You will harmonize your vibrational signature with that of the zero-state vibrational essence. It will be of resonance, not of riddance. Is this of understanding now?

It is of essence to move forward. But you see, at some point you have to STOP, readjust, and then move forward again from a different place.

11.   We've changed our life rhythms. Rather, our new technological environment has altered our rhythms, and we've not had sufficient time biologically, as well as psychologically, to adjust. What would you say about this?

It is true. Technology has created dissonance in such a way that your evolution has been stunted. You see, it has to be that unified nudging, and you have not been inclined to feel that nudge. Now, it has to be more so of a blow rather than a nudge. You see, technological advancement will always serve humanity from its own state of consciousness, and at present it is still very much splintered to really make it of use. You can see from the worldwide web that it is all about connections and widening your communicative scope, your consciousness. Is this of understanding, for you see it is always relational?

We would also like to say but one thing - you see, it is never about ridding life of yourselves: sitting upon a hilltop void of self, void of world, no. But what it is, is to take away the false self that has been socially constructed. Let that go, allow this vibrational essence to flow through your being, birthing a new vibrational signature - a non-splintered one, a unified one. It is almost like taking off the band-aid on a cut, allowing the body to harmonize and heal. This is what we come forth; for not to have no self - although there really is no self - but to allow a more harmonized self. The birthing of a whole new humanity, one consciousness at a time, one vibrational alignment at a time. We are grateful for this communication and will continue as long as need be. With much Love and Light – Abe.

12.   Thank you, Abe. What you say sounds similar to what was said by the Indian mystic Aurobindo. He referred to the 'Supramental' or 'Overmind' and how we need to allow it to manifest through us - to 'bring in' this unified consciousness. What can you say about this?

It is so. A collaboration, as you would say, in your physical existence of minds. But mind is vibrational signature and vibrational signature is caused by the vibrational resonance, to create pathways within the brain. This is exactly what it is like outside of you - like a web of consciousness within, it so now needs to be allowed without also. Is this of understanding?

13.	So, are you saying that one of the functions of the human being is to collaborate with the unified consciousness, to develop resonance, and allow pathways for a pure consciousness to manifest? That is, to form more pathways of connection and unity?

Yes, it is. It is about widening your field of consciousness - opening up the dolls of being contained within another and another until you see 'but oh yes, I am that and that is but me, I were just encased.' Is this of understanding?

14.	Humanity is mapping the world and the cosmos like never before. We are seeking deep into the oceans. We are mapping the entire solar system, and our telescopes search deep into the cosmos. What will we find if we don't first find ourselves?

Nothing. You can only ever but find yourselves - but if so coming from a splintered mind, you are finding everything else but yourselves. Is this of understanding?

15.	Many people - from scientists to philosophers – are saying that we are entering a post-human era. How can we be going 'post' human if we haven't yet discovered what being human truly means?

This is why it is of utmost importance to strip it back, figure out this part of yourselves in which has been closed off. In the realization of yourselves you see all that you are and all that you have ever been - and that is the whole thing. And from this point new pathways will be open, new things will be seen, new resonance. But see this, they will be new to the eyes that have not yet been open but old news to those that have been awake. Love and Light – Abe.

16.   It can be said that the human is both 'being and becoming' – this seems to suggest a combination between a state of rest and a state of evolving. Is there some truth to this?

Yes. It is always this so - you have to be in tune with what you are to allow these subtle shifts to take course within you and create new horizons outside of you.

17.   Can you give some examples when the pure consciousness was manifested upon our planet?

It is always a flow - but I realize you are asking who or what has brought it forth before. And we can say that there has been many, and this has always been in relation to that of the pathways that are so created at the time of being. It is really manifested in all that you do. But see this, it is but always dependent upon the pathways within the vibrational signature of how this manifests in your world. This is why we are coming forth - to allow a recalibration, a reset if you will. To harmonize what is available to you at your next evolutionary step of creating vibrational pathways - not only within but without too. Is this of understanding?

18.		By recalibrating our resonance and alignment,
		are we also physically re-wiring connections in our
		brain? Is this what is meant by our potential for
		neuro- plasticity?

It is so, yes. You are not only doing so with the brain but also
DNA is receiving this new shift, this new alignment. All is in
conversation - it just depends upon what conversation it is,
and what you are so to allow. Love and Light – Abe.

19.		Would this mean that old patterns or neural
		connections will become obsolete because they
		are no longer of resonance? If this is so, then this
		would also cause habit patterns in our lives to
		be broken down too, wouldn't it?

Yes, this is so. Connections will be lost within and this will also
affect your outer lives too. This may look like loss, but it is only
opening up for new pathways to be formed which are more of
resonation to your being and to that of which is trying to
manifest in form. Love and Light – Abe.

20.		You have spoken much about humanity's
		splintered mind. What other things do we need to
		change or shift in order to better harmonize with
		our future?

Firstly, this unification of self - that is it. We do not want to give
but a long 'to do' list. Just this for now - find this. Love and
Light – Abe.

	The future is a complex subject. We understand
	you may not wish to disclose too much – yet what
	can you tell us about humanity's future?

It is always in but relation to that of which you have unified. For the path, for so long, has been one of restriction of consciousness. You are on the other side of becoming a round-about circle, and when but this phase has come once you have readjusted, reset. You are but setback on becoming. Take, for example, a child riding a bike - you gently direct and readjust for the child can take this or leave it. It is completely up to them and in this it creates the paths. Is this of understanding?

You see, it is very simple; and by labelling and scrutinizing something you then loose the very meaning. It is to be seen, to be watched, to be felt - for in this the secrets of the universe are revealed. And in this you realise that there was never a secret to be found - you just had to allow yourself to fall back into resonance, into you. Is this of understanding?

22.	You have mentioned about becoming
	harmonized to what is available to us at our next
	evolutionary step. Could you explain more what
	you mean by this?

Yes, but of course. You see, it is really about allowing - like the wave that has a high and a low, a rest and peak. It could be likened of action and inaction; this is allowing resonance. Knowing but when to rest and see, and readjust, before taking off into action. This is but the lower point of the vibrational wave, and to fuss and fight and to have to constantly keep it in a straight line of resonance you are in hindsight flat-lining life. It is a constant balance between the two, and to know when is where you have to re-attune yourselves. Is this of understanding?

You see, there are many belief systems and constructs that tell you to pick a side and stick with it, and life does not move in such a way. Life is a wave of vibrational potential.

23.   Following on from what you say about the high and low points of vibrational wave. Does this suggest that currently humanity is at a 'lower point' on the vibrational wave? That higher energies are coming that will shift this trajectory?

It is to say that. But do not take higher and lower as, to say, in your own constructs, sense of the words, for they are of equal resonance. But yes, you are but in a dip. It is the time to readjust, realign, and then move forth. For if not so, you will continue with this path of resistance and constant action. Is this of understanding?

You see, in the constant path of action you are but killing life. You are straightening it out, and also it goes for the other end of constant rest. It has to be of resonance - of movement, of rest, of breath. Love and Light – Abe.

That energy is always there - it is just that the evolution is one of consciousness now. It always, but always, has to be in resonance to the mechanism or organism that is receiving such vibrations. Is this of understanding?

24.   What is the source for this 'dip' in vibrational resonance - is it due to cosmic conditions? Is it that the organism (humanity) has not evolved in line to receive the vibrations of consciousness - are we in need of a nudge?

It is such this. But also, just local. For like we say, there are at this point contained vibrational waves and dips which are of locality - physical points like the synapses. You see, the vibrational essence or resonance that would connect the two have to be of resonance. The connections cannot, and will not, be made until your own individual pathways have been readjusted, reset, and reunited. Is this of understanding now?

We are but the nudge. But you are also of that too. Love and Light – Abe.

25.   So, until this readjustment and realignment can occur, humanity is, in a   sense, 'cut off' from the full cosmic connection and communication. As a species, we need to develop our collective synapse in order to create the pathway, the bridge. Is this a fair description?

It is, yes. At some point you need to stop - gather and rest, readjust, and realign with this wave, this vibration. It is like when you sing too fast in a song and get ahead of yourselves, or are too slow and therefore you are still far behind. It is of a mutual emergence. Is this of understanding?

A mirror, a dance of vibrational resonance. Love and Light – Abe.

26.   And this readjustment can begin with individuals? Does it require a 'tipping point' - a sufficient mass - rather than a whole species adjustment?

It has to be started there from the beginning. Like we say, back to the bare bones of things - for there is but too much noise, too much contamination. Of course, it will always be so - that the more weight in the scale will tip the balance just that tiny bit. What we want to say, that indeed it does not have to be the whole species but a balance of sorts. Is this of understanding?

You see, it will be this way - and more and more will follow. Like the cycle we talk of, you're stepping into a dip, whereas the old action-orientated resonance is too much - it is going around again to rebalance. But see this, it will always be a kind of tug-of-war to keep balance. For you see, when someone likes a certain food they would want more and more, and in this get tired of it at some point. It will not resonate, so it will go back to zero and rethink about the choices. This can be likened to that of this kind of scenario. Is this of resonance to you? Can you see that in which we speak? For it is always a becoming. Love and Light – Abe.

27.   How do you sense this will unfold? Personally, we have a positive view on humanity's future. How does Abe consider the readjustment process, or period?

It will be one of discomfort, for all readjustment is uncomfortable. For if you have been sitting in a certain position for a while, when you come to move to another position it is of discomfort, is it not? But this discomfort remains to be seen as to how tightly you hold on to out-dated paradigms and how allowing you are to this vibration. That's why, you see, it is a time to stop and see. Is this of understanding?

28.   Will this discomfort period cover the rest of what we call the 21st century? Or will it be a shorter span? (We realize it is somewhat difficult to talk about time lengths).

You see this, that it is so. But if you are able to tip the balance just a little, we would see this be happening within the next 10 years. But see this, it will be a tug-of-war between what is and what wants to become. And could even see this time shortened, so long as people can recalibrate. Is that of understanding?

29.	Hello Abe. We wish to clarify by asking our first question again - can you explain 'who' is Abe?

We are glad to come forth and clarify, and we see that we have but already described what we are - but maybe a deeper knowing is of essence here? You see, we have to be careful as to not explain our way into thinking that you and we are of any difference at all, not at core. We are but your original state of being, it is just that you do so have conditions of a body, which creates different vibratory interference in a way. For you see, we do not have a physical body and are not of a point of place - only but when in communication with you both. The reason we are to come forth as Abe is because we are but a focal point of constricted consciousness, shortened to become, or seem to become, separate - but we are not. You are just being receptive to this conscious flow - and in this it has taken form, in a sense, through yourselves. See it as a radio station in which you would like to listen to. You tune-in to certain channel, but you see you have but no preference and it is allowing more to come forth. Like we say, Abe is just a shortened constriction of the whole thing - an abbreviation of pure consciousness. Is this of understanding now?

30.	Is there anything Abe would wish to say to 'finalize' this book material - perhaps as an end message to the reader?

We would like to say that we are grateful for this communication and that there is always space and time, we are not in a great hurry. But we do so feel that this information is of importance now. People are the key connection, are the source, and unification is really what you are. You see, for something to become anything it starts with nothing. When all is seen that this is but the cycle of life then you could probably loosen up a little and allow all that you are to flow through you - unrestricted by what you have been conditioned to think, to be. The time is now to understand your extraordinary existence and at the same time your very ordinary existence - this is true unification of being. And you will see that you start to breathe again - you start to live again, and you start to love again. What a journey. You see, in this you realise you have come but full circle - but this time you are awake, you are alive. With much Love and Light - Abe.

GET IN TOUCH

Would you like to ask ABE a question?

Visit us at https://www.thewaybackhome.one/

or email us at:
contact@thewaybackhome.net